Nigel Holmes

CRAZY
COMPETITIONS

Crazy Competitons

100 Weird and Wonderful Rituals
around the World

In 2001, Takeru Kobayashi won **Nathan's Hot Dog Eating Contest** by downing 50 of them in 12 minutes.*

That event and two others were really the genesis of this book. (The two others were **rolling big cheeses** down a steep hill in England, and running after them; and **throwing dead rats** in Spain, and trying to hit other people with them.) I was hooked on the odd things we do. Could there possibly be enough to fill a book? 100 perhaps? Yes, easily!

So what's in *Crazy Competitions*? It's easier to tell you what's not.

To non-cricket-playing nations, **cricket** is an awfully slow (hours-long), extremely high-scoring sport. To fully conscious people, **boxing** (where the point is to knock the opponent unconscious by punching him or her in the head) is just cruel and danger-ous. To many Americans, the version of **football** played there (which leaves many of its players with fatal brain injuries after their careers are over) should actually be banned, or at least have its rules overhauled.

Why aren't those events in this book? They are surely just as odd as **Bog Snorkelling, Worm Charming,** or the **Night of the Radishes.** The line had to be drawn somewhere. Organized sports with professional teams, or individuals whose job is their sport, are different from the largely amateur, often splendid, mostly once-a-year oddities you'll find here. So cricket, football, boxing, and other events and sports like them, aren't included.

Some that are included are so odd, if not incredible, that it's difficult to believe they actually take place. (To test your own credulity, **one of the 100 events in this book is in fact completely made up.**)

On the contents pages, **you'll find official urls** for many of the festivals or "sports," so you can read more about them, and see photos in case you think my drawings don't do them justice. Since some of the 100 events are little more than quirky fundraisers for charity, existing solely due to the enthusiasm of very enthusiastic people, it's possible that some of them may not happen in the years to come. My apologies if your favorite is not happening any more. Just add it to the list of historical oddities that show us how very odd we once were, and apparently still are.

*That amazing feat set by Kobayashi in 2001 doubled the record set just one year earlier. The number of hot dogs gradually went up, and in 2017 the world record reached 72 eaten—in only 10 minutes.

Americas
and the
Caribbean

Canada

United States

Mexico

Cayman Islands

El Salvador

Colombia

Ecuador

Brazil

Bolivia

Argentina

1
2
3
4
5
6
7
8
9
10
11
12
13
14
15
16
17

*A stone skipping contest is held
on Easdale Island, Scotland,
see contest number 19.

5

Europe

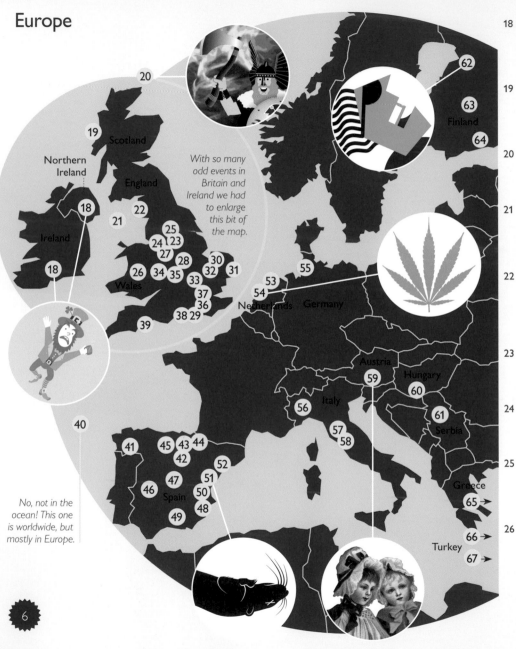

With so many odd events in Britain and Ireland we had to enlarge this bit of the map.

No, not in the ocean! This one is worldwide, but mostly in Europe.

Northern Ireland

Scotland

England

Ireland

Wales

Netherlands

Germany

Austria

Hungary

Italy

Serbia

Spain

Greece

Turkey

Finland

19
20
18
18
22
21
25
24 23
27
26 34 35 28
33
32 30
31
37
36
38 29
39
40
53
54
55
59
56
57
58
60
61
41
45 43 44
42
52
47 51
46
50
48
49
65 →
66 →
67 →
62
63
64

6

18 Ból an Bhóthair
Road bowling in Ireland and Northern Ireland, year-round
www.irishroadbowling.ie
p. 50

19 Stone Skimming
Easdale Island, Scotland*,
September
www.uphellyaa.org
p. 24

20 Up Helly Aa
Fire festival in Lerwick,
Scotland, January
p. 52

21 World Tin Bath Championships
Isle of Man, England, July
www.castletown.org.im/tinbaths
p. 54

22 World Gurning Championships
Egremont, England,
September
www.egremontcrabfair.com
p. 56

23 Welly Wanging
Upperthong, England,
summer
p. 58

24 Worm Charming
Willaston, England, June
www.wormcharming.com
p. 60

25 Coal Carrying
Gawthorpe, England,
Easter Monday
www.gawthorpemaypole.org.uk
p. 62

26 Bog Snorkelling
Llanwrtyd Wells, Wales,
August
p. 64

*The world record was set in the US, see contest number 7.

7

Africa,
Asia and
Oceania

Mongolia 80

Japan

81

92 91

China   South Korea   93 90

89

94

82   95

74

75

India

76   78

77

83

Thailand   84

79   Sri Lanka

Philippines

88

85   Borneo   87

Sumatra   86

Mali   Niger

68   69

70

Togo

South Sudan   Ethiopia

71   71

Tanzania

72 ┄ Zanzibar
Island

96

Australia

Vanuatu 100 →

97   New
Zealand

98   99

South
Africa

73

Americas
and the Caribbean

Arctic Man
Ski race

Alaska
US
Canada

**Hoodoo Mountains
(near Lake Summit), US**
April

In 1985, two men in a bar (where else?) made a bet about a race down a nearby mountain. Now it's an annual festival that 13,000 people come to watch. The event is referred to as "Burning Man's* cold ass brother," and "the world's craziest ski race." Before it starts, there's a parade of snowmobiles (more than 1,000 of them), which is listed in *The Guinness Book of Records*.

*Burning Man is an arts festival that takes place in Black Rock Desert, Nevada, in August.

Racers compete in two-person teams: a skier or snowboarder and a snowmobiler.

1

The skier descends 1,700 ft (520 m) from the summit…

2

then **grabs a tow rope attached to his teammate's snowmobile,** which pulls the skier up a second mountain at 80+ mph (130+ km/h).

Apart from watching the race, you'll have a chance to eat reindeer-on-a-stick, and see the ◄······ **Northern Lights** when you go to Arctic Man. It's cold in Alaska, so you'll probably drink a whole lot as well.

3 At the top of the second mountain, **the skier lets go of the tow rope and descends** 1,200 ft (365 m) to the finish line.

4 The race is 5.5 mi (8.9 km) long, and the winner's prize is around USD 60,000. Olympic and world record skiers are among the contenders.

International **Hair-Freezing** Contest

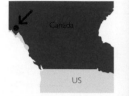

Canada

US

Whitehorse,
Canada
February

This crazy
Hair-Freezing
Contest started
in 2011. It's part
of the Yukon
Sourdough
Rendezvous
that's been held
in Whitehorse
for more than
50 years.

Here's what you do:

1 **Soak** in the hot springs. The water is 104° F (40 °C). **Dip your head** in it.

2 **Stand up** and let the **cold** air (it's around -22° F (-30° C) **freeze** your hair.

3 Keep your **ears** warm if you can (it's not easy)!

4 As your hair freezes, you can **form it into wild shapes.**

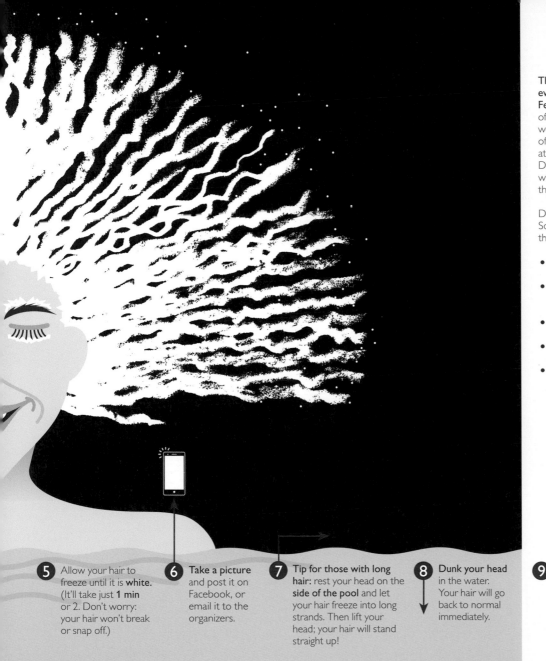

The main hair-freezing event takes place in February, but because of the variability of the weather any picture of your frozen hair taken at the hot springs from December through March will be considered for the competition.

During the Yukon Sourdough Rendezvous there are **other events:**

- Snow Carving Contest

- Texas Hold'em Poker Contest

- Fiddle Show

- Burlesque Show

- **Just for men:** Sourdough Sam Contest This involves lip synching, a dance-floor strip tease, and a kielbasa-eating contest—in drag.

5 Allow your hair to freeze until it is **white.** (It'll take just **1 min** or 2. Don't worry: your hair won't break or snap off.)

6 Take a picture and post it on Facebook, or email it to the organizers.

7 Tip for those with long hair: rest your head on the **side of the pool** and let your hair freeze into long strands. Then lift your head; your hair will stand straight up!

8 Dunk your head in the water. Your hair will go back to normal immediately.

9 **Winners** are announced in March. First prize is CAD 750.

15

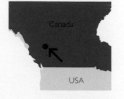

Chetwynd,
Canada
June

The four-day
competition
began in 2005.
Carvers from
Australia, Japan,
Nigeria, and
Denmark, as well
as Canada and
the US, are
among recent
contestants.

Twelve professional carvers are invited to take part.

First, there's the **log draw.** Huge trunks of Western Red Cedar are trucked
to Chetwynd from Campbell River on Vancouver Island, some 550 mi (885 km) away,
and are cut into 12 pieces of approximately the same size.

If carvers don't
like the log they've
drawn, they are
allowed to swap
it with one
from a willing
co-competitor.

**The carvers have until the morning of the fourth day
to work on their sculpture,** fashioning the cedar trunks into
whatever they want. Animals are popular subjects.

Eighty-eight carvings from previous years are displayed in Chetwynd.
But it's not a big place (population: 3,100) so the town's mayor is concerned that
the cost of maintaining the work may mean in future they'll have to send
new sculptures to neighboring towns.

Another major chainsaw carving competition, the Husky Team World Cup, takes place in Mulda, Germany, annually in May.

Unlike the single-participant Chetwynd event, the six invited teams at the Husky Cup are given a theme (for instance, a medieval hunt, with lifesize animal and human figures).

Other tools (such as drills, grinders and sanders) may be used in addition to chainsaws of all sizes, but some carvers like to make their art solely with a chainsaw.

Competitors must use the log they draw (or swap) and nothing else, but they can cut the wood up and join pieces together to make their finished carvings.

Some darken their carvings in places by burning them with blowtorches.

After judging on the fourth day, there's a quick-carve contest, resulting in smaller pieces, many of which can be bought right there.

17

Pig-N-Ford Races

Tillamook, US
August

Sometime in the early 1920s, someone in a Model T Ford somewhere in Oregon saw a pig running wild. The pig was caught, and an idea was born.

In 1925, the first Pig-N-Ford race was run at the Tillamook County Fair. It's been popular ever since.

To take part you have to be a member of the Tillamook County Model T Pig-N-Ford Association. Memberships (and cars) are passed down through families. Only occasionally does a coveted membership open up, and even then it's by invitation only.

1 There are **five cars** in each race. Drivers line them up in the middle of the track and switch off their engines.

2 The drivers line up at the outer edge of the track. **When the starter fires his gun, they race across the track…**

3 to the inner edge, where **they grab a 20 lb (9 kg) pig** from the drivers' designated pens.

4 Drivers run back to their cars, **start their engines with a hand crank,** jump in with the squealing, wriggling pig gripped tightly under their arm, **and drive off.**

In the early years of the race, drivers used their everyday road cars, but today the Model Ts are stripped down to the bare minimum. No modern tweaks are allowed to replacement parts.

Some of the cars from 1925 are still runnning in the races.

5 After one lap of the racetrack (the Averill Arena horse-racing track), drivers must stop their engines, put the first pig back in its pen and **pick up a second one.**

6 Then, they have to crank start the engine, jump in with the new pig, and drive **a second lap.**

7 They stop after the second lap, kill the engine again, grab a third pig, crank the engine, and do **a third lap.**

8 That's it. After passing the finish line, the **first driver to put the third pig back in its pen wins.**

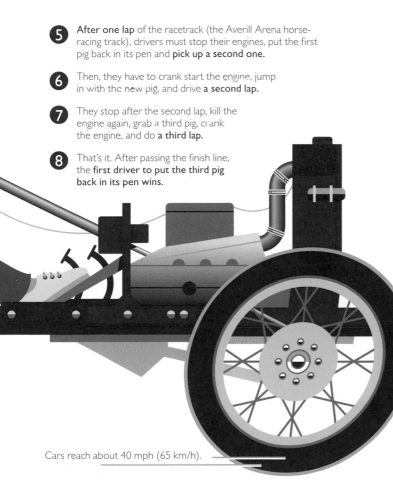

Cars reach about 40 mph (65 km/h).

There are **preliminary races** on the Thursday, Friday, and Saturday of the fair. The winners of those races compete for the **World Championship Final on Saturday.**

All this is in addition to the ingredients of a traditional American county fair: sideshows, rollercoasters, big wheels, and food. Lots of food—including pork, both deep-fried and bacon-wrapped.

Air Sex

US

↗

**Throughout
the US**
Year-round

Although a little
more racy than
most of the other
competitions in
this book, the
Air Sex World
Championship had to
be included—it's just
too much fun to
leave out. The first
event was held in
2006 in Japan and
since 2009 versions
of the show have
taken place in
bars and clubs all
over the US.

Anyone can enter,
but there are rules:

1 **No nudity**
is allowed.

2 There
must be an
**imaginary
person or
object**
involved. ⋯⋯⋯⋯⋯⋯

3 **All orgasms
must be
simulated.**
"When you
come on stage,
you may not
come on stage."

4 Contestants
have **2 min**
to perform
a routine.

5 **Contestants perform to music.** They can email an MP3 to the organizer (in the US it's chris@gmail.com).

6 They can bring a CD with them on the night, or they can choose from the Air Sex music catalog provided by the organizers.

7 A panel of comics and sex professionals judges the first round, and the **audience chooses the eventual winner.**

8 The winners of regional events meet for a **final show that takes place in a different city each year.** The top three winners at this show perform together on stage, and the audience chooses the champion.

Performance tips

- Humor works better than outright porn.

- Simulating rape is just wrong (and your air sex act will be stopped.)

- Moaning and speaking is allowed, but silence is golden.

- Looking hot is not as good as looking silly.

Watch
Air Sex: The Movie to see people performing.

Sex *in* the air

Following terrorist attacks, it has become harder to join the **Mile High Club:** airlines have beefed up security, and double trips to the toilet look suspicious. But you can buy packages for "intimate experiences" aboard small (typically six-seater) specially customized planes, where it's just you, your partner and a discreet pilot (who wears noise-cancelling headphones).

It takes between 5 and 10 min for the pilot to climb to 5,280 ft, or 1 mi (1,600 m). Then the seat belts can be unfastened…

Angola Prison Rodeo

St. Francisville, US
3rd weekend in April, and every Sunday in October

Called the **Wildest Show in the South**, the prison rodeo started in **1965** as entertainment for inmates of the Louisiana State Penitentiary.

It was such a success that seating capacity for visitors was increased over the years, and a new stadium was built in **2000** with enough room for **7,500** spectators.

There are **nine events**, including:

- **Wild Cow Milking**
  Teams try to catch a cow and get some milk from it as it runs around the arena.

- **Bareback Riding**
  (a classic rodeo competition)
  Any inmate who can ride the bucking bronco for **8 sec** is a winner.

- **Bull Riding**
  (another classic event)
  If an inmate can stay on the 2,000 lb (900 kg) bull for **6 sec** he earns the title All-Around Cowboy.

Since the prisoners aren't skilled riders, they wear **crash helmets and padded vests** for all events.

Of all the rodeo events, this one is perhaps the oddest:

- **Convict Poker**
  Four convicts sit at a table holding cards while a 1,500 lb (680 kg) bull charges at them. The **last man to remain seated at the table wins.**

There are about 5,000 convicts in the Angola prison. Three-quarters of them are serving a life sentence without parole. Eight hundred prisoners make **furniture,** and other **arts and crafts,** which are for sale to the public at the rodeo.

Inmates also work on the prison farm, which at 18,000 acres (7,300 ha) is the size of Manhattan. It grows cotton, wheat, and corn and is on the site of a former plantation that used Africans as slave labor.

The name of the prison is a reference to **Angola in Africa** and the people who were brought from there to be sold in America.

23

World Record
Stone Skipping

US

Red Bridge, US
September, 2013*

Not a competition, just an amazing thing. (And one that anyone can try.)

This event measures **how many skips** .... the stone makes.

The world record is **88 skips,*** set by Kurt "Mountain Man" Steiner. (The previous record was 65.)

World Stone Skimming Championships

Scotland

England

Easdale Island, Scotland
Last Sunday in September

Started in 1983, this one's a real competition.

*Records get broken. This was the stone-skipping record when we went to press.

This event measures **how far** .... the stone travels.

Distances covered in the Easdale event reach about **195 ft (60 m).**

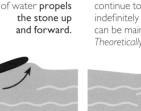

I could only fit 44 skips into this drawing—half of Kurt's amazing record.

What do we call it?
(A selection from the long list of countries' names for the event.)

America	**stone skipping**
Britain	**stone skimming**
Bulgaria	**frogs**
Finland	**throwing a sandwich**
Hungary	**making it walk like a duck**
Japan	**cutting water**
Mongolia	**making the rabbit leap**
Russia	**baking pancakes**

WWII Dam Busters
In 1943, Britain's Royal Air Force used a principle similar to stone skipping when they **dropped cylindrical bombs** from Lancaster bombers over German bodies of water. The bombs **bounced across the water**, avoiding vertical torpedo nets, until they hit German dams. The bombs sank and **exploded underwater**, damaging the targets.

How it works
The best stone is smooth, thin, weighs about 5 oz (150 g), and has a surface area of **4–6 in² (10–15 cm²)**.* It can be roundish or triangular. The bigger the surface area, the more lift it'll get out of the water.

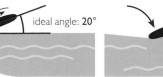

Spin the stone as you throw it, with a flick of the wrist.

ideal angle: **20°**

The movement of water **propels the stone up and forward.**

Theoretically, it will continue to skip indefinitely if the speed can be maintained. *Theoretically.*

*The Easdale Championships limit the size of the stone to 3 in² (7.5 cm²), and it must be a piece of slate from the quarry.

Nathan's
Hot Dog
Eating
Contest

New York, US
July 4

Legend has it that four immigrants held a hot dog eating contest in **1916**. It's been a recorded event since 1972. Today's stomach-turning (and filling) spectacle takes place on America's Independence Day, on Coney Island.

Past winners are automatically invited, plus about 20 other contestants who have qualified at eating events earlier in the year. On this day, they compete for prizes totalling USD 40,000.

26

Below: **72 hot dogs,** the amount the current world record holder* **Joey Chestnut** ate in the 2017 contest.

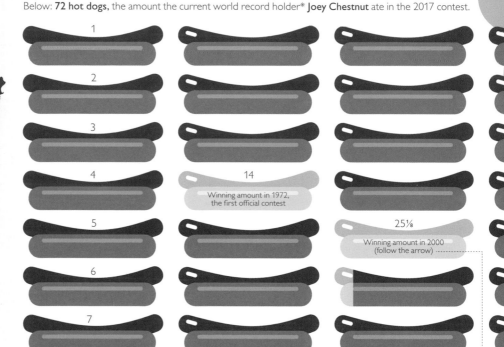

1
2
3
4
5
6
7
8
9
10

14
Winning amount in 1972, the first official contest

25⅛
Winning amount in 2000 (follow the arrow) ·····

20
30

The competition is organized by **Major League Eating (MLE),** in association with the **International Federation of Competitive Eating (IFOCE).**

Each contestant has a designated **scorekeeper** who displays the number of hot dogs eaten. The allotted time is **10 min.**

The winner is the one who eats, *and keeps down,* the most hot dogs. **No "reversal of fortune"** (vomiting) is allowed.

*Correct when we went to press.

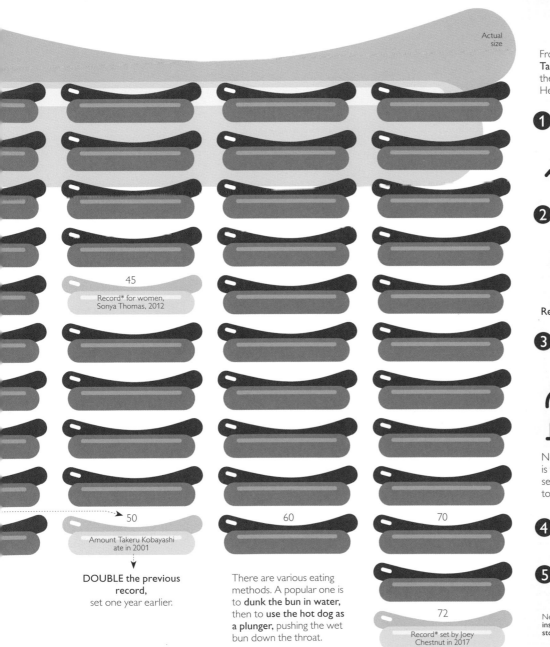

45

Record* for women,
Sonya Thomas, 2012

→ 50

Amount Takeru Kobayashi
ate in 2001

↓

**DOUBLE the previous
record,**
set one year earlier.

60

70

72

Record* set by Joey
Chestnut in 2017

There are various eating
methods. A popular one is
to **dunk the bun in water,**
then to **use the hot dog as
a plunger,** pushing the wet
bun down the throat.

Actual
size

From 2001 to 2006,
Takeru Kobayashi was
the champion eater.
Here's how he **trained:**

1 Jog for hours.
(Shrinks stomach.)

2 Drink lots of water.
(Expands stomach.)

Repeat 1 and 2 a few times.

3 Eat low-fat, high-fiber
food, such as cabbage.
(Stays in the stomach
a long time
before
breaking
down.)

Normally, when the stomach
is full, its muscles stretch and
send **"stop eating"** messages
to the brain.

4 Practice ignoring
those messages.
(This is the hard part.)

5 Fast on the day of
the contest.

Next page:
**inside the
stomach.**

27

More about eating hot dogs and a whole lot of other food, competitively.

OK, the question everyone asks is: **What happens immediately after the contest is over?** (Or to put it another way, where does the food go? Or even: which end does the food come out?)

None of the contestants are talking. And that's understandable because they have just been paid by the companies making the food they've consumed. It wouldn't be a good marketing move for the audience to see what actually happens to the food.

But the food has to go *somewhere*. An unconfirmed rumor states that all the contestants vomit. Thankfully, it happens out of sight.

When we eat, the **epiglottis** swivels down to stop food from going into the **windpipe.**

Being thin is a definite advantage because there's less fat to stop the stomach from expanding.

Want to be a competitive eater? A few facts to digest:

The best eaters learn to **relax the esophagus** so that it will expand and take in more food.

Normal stomach capacity is about 3.3 lb (1.5 kg).

72 hot dogs, buns and water weigh about **18 lb (8 kg).**

Training the stomach to **expand beyond its normal size** is important. (See Kobayashi's training regime on the previous page.)

72 hot dogs is **26,250 calories.** (US health officials' daily recommended amount is 2,300 calories.)

8 kg
18 lb

Not just hot dogs

Here's a partial list of competitive eating contests organized by Major League Eating.

Key:
selected record holders ----
amount eaten, time taken ----
(time not always recorded)

Ice Cream
Joey Chestnut
1.8 gal (6.8 l), 6 min

Rice Balls
Takeru Kobayashi
20 lb (9.1 kg), 30 min

Peas
Eric Booker
9.5 lb (4.3 kg)

Mars Bars
Pat Bertoletti
38, 5 min

Lobster Meat
Sonya Thomas
44 lobsters,
11.3 lb (5 kg), 12 min

Mayonnaise
Oleg Zhornitsky
8 lb (3.6 kg)

Nigiri Sushi
Tim Janus
141 pieces, 6 min

Brain Tacos
Joey Chestnut
54, 8 min

Spam
Richard LeFevre
6 lb (2.7 kg), 12 min

Cupcakes
Tim Janus
48, 8 min

Sweet Corn
Yasir Salem
47 cobs, 12 min

Boysenberry Pie
Joey Chestnut
18.3 lb (8.3 kg), 8 min

Deep Fried Asparagus
Joey Chestnut
12.5 lb (5.7 kg), 10 min

Hard-boiled Eggs
Joey Chestnut
141, 8 min

Pasta
Matt Stonie
10 lb (4.5 kg), 8 min

Twinkies
Joey Chestnut
121, 6 min

Butter
Don Lerman
7 x 0.25 lb (0.1 kg) sticks,
5 min

Birthday Cake
Matt Stonie
14.5 lb (6.6 kg), 8 min

Pommes Frites
Cookie Jarvis
2.9 lb (1.3 kg), 10 min

Oysters
Sonya Thomas
564 oysters (47 dozen),
8 mins

Bacon
Matt Stonie
182 strips (rashers), 5 min

Heart-shaped Chocolates
Pat Bertoletti
2 lb (1 kg), 7 min

Slugburgers
Matt Stonie
43, 10 min
(Slugburgers are beef
with bread filler,
deep fried.)

plus: Pickles
Jalapeño Peppers
Grits
Peanut Butter
  and Jelly Sandwiches
Frozen Yogurt
Matzah Balls
Pork Rolls
Bratwurst
Pumpkin Pie
Pancakes
Pierogis
Fish Tacos
Rocky Mountain
  Oysters
Cannoli
Doughnuts
Chilis
Shrimp
Salmon Chowder
Funnel Cake
Calamari
Clams
Rhubarb Pie
Fried Okra
Turkey
Grilled Cheese
  Sandwiches
Tamales
Burritos
Grapes
Kale Burgers
Ribs
Gumbo
Chicken Wings
Garlicky Greens
Strawberry Shortcakes
Popcorn
Key Lime Pie
Corn Dogs
Salty Ball Potatoes
Pizza
Watermelon
Tacos
Peeps
Meat Pies
Pigs' Feet and Knuckles
Corned Beef on Rye
Apple Pie
Crab Cakes
Shrimp Wontons
Pastrami Sandwiches
Baked Beans
Sweet Potato Casserole
Toasted Ravioli
Turducken (a chicken inside
  a duck inside a turkey)

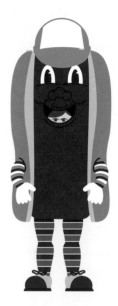

Friendly hot dogs roam the New York City competition venue. (Often obscuring spectators' views!)

29

Mexico

Día de los Muertos
The Day of the Dead
Throughout Mexico
(and elsewhere in the world)
October 31 to November 3

Several traditions are connected with this three-day public holiday. To honor the dead, people build *ofrendas*, private altars decorated with candles, skulls made of sugar, marigolds, memorabilia, and the deceased's favorite food and drink.

Some of the altars are built at home, but people also **go to cemeteries and make elaborate altars** near their loved ones' graves. They hope to **meet the souls of the dead** and that they will hear the prayers and stories told by the living. It is believed that when the **souls eat the food offerings** first so that when the living eat them later, they have no nutritional value.

Recently, the celebrations have become more like **Halloween** in the US. In Mexican cities, young people **dress up like this** and go from door to door collecting small sugar skulls, sweets, and money.

30

In most regions of Mexico, **November 1 is the day to honor the memory of dead children** (Día de los Inocentes, or Día de los Angelitos), while **November 2 is for dead adults** (Día de los Muertos), but many towns have different ways to celebrate and honor their dead.

This 1910 image by **José Guadalupe Posada** of a female skeleton dressed only in a fancy hat is often associated with the Día de los Muertos, and is known as *La Calavera Catrina* (The Elegant Skull). Posada was satirizing native Mexicans who imitated aristocratic European dress styles, and wore makeup **to make their skin whiter.**

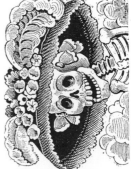

Noche de Rábanos
Night of the radishes

Mexico

Oaxaca, Mexico
December 23

Oaxaca has a tradition of wood carving, but in this event roughly 100 local farmers and others carve oversized radishes.

There's also a competition for sculptures made with corn husks and dried flowers.

One year in the mid 1700s, the radish crop in Oaxaca was so abundant that lots of the veggies were left in the ground where they grew, and grew some more.

A couple of friars pulled some up, and displayed them in the Christmas market.

Pretty soon, people started to carve the radishes into religious figures and other scenes (including Day of the Dead iconography). In **1897,** the mayor of the city created a formal radish-carving contest. It's been held every year since then.

Radishes are grown specifically for the competition. Because of heavy fertilization and growth-encouraging chemical treatment, these radishes are not suitable for eating. They are left in the ground long past normal harvesting time, growing into huge, often weird, shapes.

On December 18, radishes are distributed to the roughly 100 competitors, but carving isn't allowed until the 23rd. Judging starts at 9 pm that night.

Thousands of locals and visitors wait in line to have a look at the displays. However, they start to wilt soon after being carved and the whole event is over in a few hours.

A number of **different varieties of radish** have been used in the competition. One of them, a large, completely white radish called the *criollo,* was very popular because it didn't rot, but it's no longer available. The radishes used these days are the typical red-skinned ones. The contrast between the red outside and the white inside plays a big role in the finished carvings, which are judged in different thematic groups, from traditional to modern scenes.

A grand prize of 15,000 Mexican pesos is awarded to the best traditional scene.

To make sure the tradition continues, **children aged 6 to 17** are encouraged to enter a competition of their own.

In 2014, **12 US t (10 t)** of radishes were used in the contest.

Odd shapes are often incorporated into the final carvings.

They *are* big —for radishes— at up to **21 in (54 cm)** long. Here's a human to the same scale. (Just kidding!)

Pirates Week

Florida, US

Cuba

Cayman Islands
November

This festival started in 1982. You'll see lots of would-be pirates (at least as far as their costumes are concerned), and be part of some 32 events, including a mock pirate invasion, fireworks, and crowning the Festival Queen. Just go and have fun, along with 35,000 other people ready to party.

GULF OF MEXICO

Cuba

Little Cayman   Cayman Brac

Grand Cayman

Mexico

Jamaica

CARIBBEAN SEA

Honduras

Nicaragua

The Jolly Roger. It's not been proved where the name of the pirates' flag derived from. The English word "roger" (wandering vagabond) might be the origin. Or it's named after Old Roger (another name for the devil).

Most pirates actually flew a plain black flag (the skull and crossbones was used less often). A black flag on a pirate ship meant that anyone being confronted would be allowed to surrender, and there'd be no bloodshed.

But if the ship did not surrender, the pirates would raise a **red flag**, and no mercy would be shown. The red flag was greatly feared; on seeing it, most ships surrendered immediately.

The route from the New World to Spain taken by **treasure galleons** loaded with gold and silver passed right by Grand Cayman Island.

During the Golden Age of Piracy (1650s to 1730s), **Grand Cayman's** position on the treasure-ship route was an ideal place for pirates to hide in waiting. Also, the Caymans were a good place for the captains of pirate ships to find crews for vessels they'd captured, to hide loot, and to repair their ships. And there was plenty of fresh water, wood, and turtle meat.

The English had established themselves in **Jamaica** by 1660, and they considered the Caymans to be part of their territory. But they left the three islands largely unattended, so pirates moved in.

The most infamous pirate associated with the Caymans was Edward Teach, better known as **Blackbeard** (his beard was bushy, long, and sometimes tied with colored ribbons). He was active near the Caymans for the last five years of his life, before he died in 1718.

Why eye patches?
Seamen could keep one eye adapted to the dark to help them when going from the glare of sunlight to below deck.

Arrrrrrrrrrrr!

And women?
Pirates thought it was bad luck to have a woman on board. But a few made it anyway and were reputed to be pretty brutal. **Anne Bonny** crossed to America in the early 1700s and **Cheng I Sao** commanded one of China's most feared pirate armies in the early 1800s.

Other buccaneers are George Lowther, his lieutenant Edward Low, and **Henry Morgan**. That's the Captain Morgan Seagrams named its rum after (in 1944).

Why parrots?
They are linked to pirates mostly because of R.L. Stevenson's 1883 novel *Treasure Island*. Long John Silver had a talking parrot called Captain Flint as a pet.

Why wooden legs?
Cutting off a gangrenous leg was the quickest way to save a life. Cutting was usually done by the **ship's cook**. Wood for the peg leg was plentiful: the ship was made of it.

Talk like a pirate*
Here's some stuff you would have heard aboard a pirate ship in the late 17th century.
(Actually, on *any* ship at that time; pirates didn't invent the words.)

Avast, matey!
Literally *houd vast* (hold fast); in Dutch, it meant **stop**, or **hold still**. Matey means mate.

Scuttlebutt
A butt is a wooden cask, and you scuttle it to make a hole. While pirates drank near the scuttlebutt **(cask of drinking water)**, they **gossiped** about life and rumors aboard ship.

Keel hauling
A brutal punishment. A rope was passed under the ship, and one end was attached to an offender's legs, the other to his wrists. **Thrown overboard, he was dragged beneath the ship** from one side to the other.

Grog
This is **rum diluted with water.** The water quality on board ships was not good after a long trip, so it was mixed with a little rum to hide the bad taste.

*International **Talk Like a Pirate Day** is September 19.

Las Bolas de Fuego

Fireball festival

Belize

Mexico

Guatemala

Honduras

Nicaragua

**Nejapa,
El Salvador**
August 31

When the El Playón volcano erupted in **1658**, villagers in nearby Nixapa said they saw fireballs being thrown into the air as they fled to safety.

Some thought that San Jeronimo was fighting the devil with these balls of fire.

Two preselected teams, representing good and evil, reenact San Jeronimo's fight with the devil.

The balls are bundles of rags that have been soaked in kerosene for a month or so.

Those who care about the safety of their hands wear **heavy leather gloves.**

Decorated costumes are thoroughly soaked in water before the fight. **People get burned.** Medics stand by.

The fight lasts about an hour. It's pretty dangerous for both the throwers and the unprotected crowds lining the street. No winner is declared. (Perhaps San Jeronimo's fight with the devil was unresolved.)

When stray fireballs land on the street they roll along leaving a flaming **trail of kerosene**.

Foolhardy spectators sometimes pick up the burning balls and throw them back into the action.

After the 1658 eruption, the new village, now a safe distance from the volcano, was named **Nejapa**.

El Playón erupted again in 1922. This is when Las Bolas de Fuego started and it soon became an annual celebration. There's a music festival in the daytime and the firefight begins when night falls.

Despite the risk of sustaining severe burns, the event has been described as more like a snowball fight… but with fireballs.

Carnaval de Barranquilla

**Barranquilla,
Colombia**
Starts on the
Saturday before
Ash Wednesday

**With 300-year-old
traditions, this
carnival comprises
dances, music,
and cultural
influences from
Europe, Africa, and
India. In 2003, the
event was listed
on UNESCO's
Masterpieces of
the Oral and
Intangible Heritage
of Humanity.**

There are lots of different
characters in the carnival,
but perhaps the most
beloved are the **Marimondas,**
the clowns of the show.
Their silly antics keep
everyone amused with
a healthy dose of fun
on all four days of
the festivities.

The **Marimondas'
costume** was originally
created by a man
from Barranquilla. He
couldn't afford expensive
expensive carnival
clothes so made his
own, topped by a bag
over his head with holes
for eyes and mouth,
and a peculiar long nose
hanging down from
the eyes.

Today, Marimondas
dress in the same simple
style of the original, but
in **teams of matching
bright colours.**

Marimondas embody
the carnival slogan:
*"Quien lo vive,
es quien lo goza"*
(Those who live it
are those who enjoy it.)

A Barranquilla **Carnival Queen** is chosen at the end of the year before the carnival itself (giving her plenty of time to prepare). She officiates in the **Battle of Flowers** on the first day of the carnival. It's a massive parade of floats and dancers.

On the last day, Tuesday, comes the ceremonial **burial of Joselito Carnaval.** The story goes that he got very drunk and tired from all the festivities and died on the day before Ash Wednesday. However, **he is resurrected** just in time the following year.

Fiesta de la
Mama Negra

Latacunga, Ecuador
September (to honor
the Lady of Mercy),
and November
(the Independence
of Latacunga)

Mixing indigenous,
Spanish, and
African cultures,
the fiesta celebrates
three things:

- the eruption of
the Cotopaxi
volcano in 1792.

- thanking the
Lady of Mercy for
protecting the town
from the volcano.

- the arrival of
African slaves
brought to work in
the silver mines.

Mama Negra is basically **a big parade,** with many different characters, including *pacahangueros* (folk dancers), *cholas* (indigenous dancers), *palomeras* (dove carriers), people carrying the carcasses of dead pigs, brass bands, and a lot of loud drumming.

Early in the morning, there is a **ceremony marking the change of command** from those who took part the previous year to the new main characters in the parade. These are the **Moorish King,** the **Sergeant,** the **Captain of the Guard,** the **Angel of the Star,** and **La Mama Negra.**

Leading the parade are the *huacos* (sorcerers), dressed in white and wearing striped masks. They chase bad spirits away (and tease spectators lining the route).

The *huacos* are followed by the **Angel of the Star,** who represents guidance and light. Sometimes the Angel is played by a young man, and sometimes by a young girl.

The part of **La Mama Negra** is
played by a man, who's elected each
year from the Latacunga community.
He carries a black doll, representing
his daughter, **Manuelita Baltazara,**
who symbolizes unity among the
people of Latacunga.

To some observers,
the use of **blackface**
(for La Mama Negra
and other characters)
is offensive.

But the multicultural
origins of the fiesta are
very mixed up, and the
Mama Negra character
is not intended to be seen
as a caricature of black
women. Any feelings
about race (or gender)
are subsumed in the fun
of the event.

Boi Bumbá
Beat the bull

Venezuela
Colombia
Peru
Brazil

**Parintins,
Brazil**
End of June

Migrants seeking
their fortunes during
Brazil's "rubber rush"
in the 1900s brought
with them a tale of a
bull or ox *(boi)*,
a pregnant peasant,
her husband, and
a shaman.

The festival
started in 1913 as a
street parade, but
over the years it has
added indigenous
Indian legends, drum-
ming, and music.
Different versions of
Boi Bumbá are now
held in many cities in
northern Brazil.

The original story
goes like this:

1 **Mae Caterina** ········►
and her husband
Pae Francisco were
peasants who worked
for a rich farmer.
When she became
pregnant, Mae
developed a **craving
for bull's tongue.**

Mae was
thought to be
ugly, and in
the festival her
part is usually played
by a **man in drag.**

3 The theft was discovered,
and Pae and Mae were
threatened with death
by the **rich farmer.** ·········►
But he had a dream in
which he was warned
not to kill the couple.

2 To satisfy his wife's craving, **Pae killed** one of the farmer's bulls and cut out its tongue.

Unfortunately, the farmer had just given this bull, his favorite, to his beloved daughter.

Today, the tale of Boi Bumbá is played out in the **Parintins Bumbódromo,** complete with 9 m (30 ft) tall parade floats, elaborately costumed drummers and other musicians (and plenty of female dancers who are hardly costumed at all).

The town splits into rival groups: the **Garantido** team, dressed in red and led into the Bumbódrome by a red bull, and the **Caprichoso** team with a blue bull and followers wearing blue clothing.

The teams act out their version of the story, then all participants are judged in 22 categories, including best bull, best float design, and best telling of the story.

4 With the help of a **priest and a shaman** (or, more recently, a **witch doctor,** a part played by an African-Brazilian woman), Pae and Mae were able to revive the bull. **All ended well.**

Tinku*
Fighting and dancing

Macha, Bolivia
May

Tinku is a form of ritualized combat and dancing to praise Pachamama (Mother Nature). The fights often become bloody, and deaths are not uncommon. The combat is a release of long-held tensions between the indigenous Aymara and Quechua groups.

*Tinku = violent encounter in the Aymara language

FIGHTING
The ceremonial (or combat) Tinku

Fights are not meant to be personal, and **are prearranged** between extended family units. The combat starts as fist-fighting, but rocks are often carried to add weight to the punches.

Spanish *conquistadors* made slaves of the indigenous people of what later became Bolivia, and during Tinku, men wear traditional *monteras* (helmets made of thick leather that resemble *conquistadors'* hats) as protection.

Some fighters embed pieces of **glass in their gloves.** Any blood shed during the fighting is seen as a **sacrifice to Pachamama**—to bring about fertility and a good harvest.

Unlike the dancers (opposite), fighters in the combat Tinku wear relatively subdued colors. (Those **embroidered leggings** are an exception.)

44

DANCING
The festive Tinku

This part of the event simulates ritualized combat with **crouching dancers** moving to warlike drumbeats and the music of guitars and panpipes.

As the dancers **jump from one foot to the other**, they stamp hard and raise a fist to signify the violence of the combat Tinku.

Men also dance. For this part of the event, they join the women in wearing elaborate costumes.

Because there have been fatalities, **Bolivian policemen** are never far away from the action, ready to stop combatants if one falls to the ground.

Campeonato Mundial de Baile de Tango
World tango dance tournament

Buenos Aires, Argentina
August

Established in 2003, the 18-day tango festival is the culmination of qualifying rounds held in many countries around the world.

In 2009, UNESCO declared tango an **Intangible Cultural Heritage of Humanity**, in recognition of the regional identities of European immigrants, the descendants of African slaves, and local natives called *criollos*, or creoles. (Early tango was known as *tango criollo*.)

The dance originated in the **1880s** in working-class slums on the border between Argentina and Uruguay. The name comes from either the Latin *tangere* (touch), or an African slave word *tango*, meaning a drum or place to dance.

There are **two parts** to the championship:

- *Tango de pista* (salon tango) has strict traditional *milonga** (dance) rules and moves that dancers must adhere to.

- *Tango escenario* (stage tango) has more choreographed parts and might borrow from ballet or other dance forms.

The final event is in **Luna Park,** in Buenos Aires, near the River Plate.

Roughly 800 couples compete, and many of the competition events are free for the public to watch. In 2013, the rules changed to allow **same-sex couples** to compete.

There's also a product fair with dance shoes, clothes, books, and recorded music for sale.

The traditional Argentine dance is **completely improvised**, but it does spontaneously combine many different tango elements. Both lead dancer and partner must learn these moves well, so when the leader starts a move the partner knows how to follow.

Moves include the **cross**, the **figure eight**, and **leg hooks.** The most basic is the **walk:**

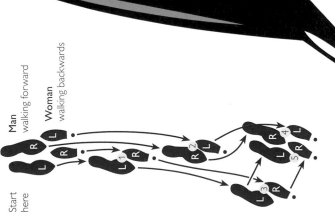

Start
here

Man
walking forward

Woman
walking backwards

*As well as a style of dance, milonga is a word for clubs and events specially for tango dancing.

One of the **codes of behavior** connected to the tango is the **cabeceo:** when a man wants to ask a woman to dance, he looks her in the eye and nods. This silent message might be sent from way across the dance floor.

The advantage is that unwanted offers can be refused without embarrassment (for both), because if the woman doesn't nod back the man is spared from walking over and being publicly rebuffed.

The national and regional champion dancers from international competitions in **Argentina, Brazil, Chile, China, the European Union, France, Japan, Russia, Turkey, the UK, and the US** are invited to take part in the final rounds of the competition.

In addition, Buenos Aires and neighboring municipalities give wild card passes to their local champions.

47

Europe

Ból an Bhóthair
Irish road bowling

Throughout the land, but mainly in County Armagh in Northern Ireland and County Cork in Ireland
Year-round

This amalgam of golf, bowling, and bocce has been played on winding roads in the Irish countryside since the 1600s.

The game is played by **two individuals or by teams of two to four.**

Since there is **no restriction on spectators standing in the road** ahead, players must shout…

ROLLING!

as a warning for them to get out of the way (like "fore" in golf).

Teammates yell "Faugh a Ballagh," which means clear the way.

The ball is thrown underarm, and leaves the player's hand at around 50 mph (80.5 km/h).

Bowlers can back up as far as 44 ft (13.5 m) from the throwing line, then sprint forward to launch the ball.

A **chalk line** (called the butt) is made on the road where the ball stops rolling after the last throw…

and the next throw starts from there.

Almost everyone oversteps the mark—it's called breaking your butt—but nobody seems to care very much.

The goal of the game is to bowl the ball along a designated course that's usually 1–3 mi (1.5–5 km) long, in as few rolls as possible.

Skilled players can complete a 1-mile course in 20 to 25 throws.

If both players (or teams) complete the course in the same number of throws, the winner is the one whose ball goes the longest distance past the finish line.

Bowling round a corner.
You are allowed to throw the ball into the air (over the corner), rather than trying to roll it all the way round.

If the ball hits the road, it's good.

If the ball lands beyond the road, it's also good; it is then moved to the nearest spot on the road.

If the ball falls short of the road, the next shot must be thrown from where it landed, in the rough.

Players have a **road shower** who positions him- or herself a few yards ahead on the road and acts like a golf caddy to help the thrower hurl the ball along the best path. He (or she) must be quick to move out of the way.

The road shower's stance

Dangerously speeding bullet

In Europe, road bowling is played in Germany and the Netherlands as well as Ireland; **in the US,** there are Irish Road Bowling associations in New York State and West Virginia.

The 1.8 lb (0.8 kg) iron or steel ball (called a bullet) is shown here actual size: 2.6 in (6.5 cm) diameter.

Leprechaun (also actual size)

51

Up Helly Aa
A fire festival

Lerwick, Shetland
Islands, Scotland
Last Tuesday
in January

Since the late
1880s, the men of
Lerwick have dressed
up as Vikings, and
marched through the
town carrying flaming
torches, which are
thrown into a replica
of a Viking longship,
burning it to cinders.

The marchers playing
Vikings for one day
are called guizers,*
and are divided into
squads of between
15 and 25 men.
The Guizer Jarl
has his own squad
of up to 70 men.

*Guizers simply means
people in disguise.

1 In the morning, **the Guizer Jarl leads the guizers** (without their torches at this point) through the town to the Market Cross…

2 where they view the **Bill,** a satirical message painted on a large board. The message, making fun of the whole event, changes each year.

3 For the rest of the morning and afternoon, the participants perform various **ceremonial activities,** and prepare for the evening's torchlit procession.

Up Helly what?
here's an explanation:

UP means ending (as in "time's up"). It refers to the ending of the Christmas holiday season.

HELLY is an old word for holy day.

AA means all. Everyone takes part.

No women allowed! The Lerwick version is the best-known of 10 Up Helly Aa celebrations in Scotland, and it's traditionally just for men.

The other nine events, listed here, are much smaller but are gender enlightened:

- Scalloway
- Nesting and Girlsta
- Uyeasound
- Northmavine
- Bressay
- Cullivoe
- Norwick
- South Mainland
- Delting

The **Guizer Jarl** is elected each year by a committee of which he must have been a member for 15 years.

4 At 7.30 pm, Lerwick's town lights are switched off and more than **1,000 torches are lit** for the procession to the **burning site** at the King George V playing field. The longship is dragged along the parade route with the Guizer Jarl standing on deck.

5 The Guizer Jarl descends from his longship, and the **1,000 flaming torches are thrown into it.**

In Viking days, when a chief died, he was laid out on his ship, which was set alight and pushed out to sea to ensure his soul was carried to **Valhalla** (Viking heaven).

World
Tin Bath
Championships

England

Castletown,
Isle of Man, UK
July

The World
Tin Bath
Championships
were started in
1971 by the
Castletown Ale
Drinkers Society
(CADS) as a way
to raise money
for charity, and to
ensure that most
competitors
get soaking wet.

There are lots of **rules**.

- You must be **able to swim** at least 148 ft (45 m).
- You must be more than **16 years old**.
- To help with recovery in case of sinking, each bath must have a **marker buoy** attached to it with a 10 ft (3 m) line.
- **Paddles** can be single- or double-bladed, must be hand-held, no longer than 5 ft (3 m), and not attached to the bath.
- No **fireworks** are allowed.

The **tin baths** themselves:

- must be **all metal**, single-hulled, and not constructed specifically for the purpose of racing;
- must be no longer than **5 ft (1.5 m)**…
- and no deeper than **16 in (40.6 cm)**;
- must have an **outrigger** attached to the bath behind the rower
  - made of wood only, 3 ft (0.9 m) long
  - with a buoyancy float* on each end, no more than 5.3 qt (5 L) capacity.

*Such as a plastic or metal container used for drinks or detergent.

- The course is 1,312 ft (400 m).

- Competitors are allowed to continue when they begin to sink, so long as no one helps them.

- The winner is the **first to finish,** or the one who covers the greatest distance **before sinking.**

Along with the men's and women's tin boat races in Castletown's Middle Harbour, there are **other events** designed to get competitors wet:

- Attempts at **human-powered flight** (p. 88). All fail miserably, to the delight of the crowd. (This event could simply be called jumping into the harbor.)

- A **zip line** with an inflated rubber raft as a target in the water halfway across the harbor. The idea is to let go of the rope and land in the raft. (Most land in the water.)

55

World
Gurning
Championships

Egremont, England
September

Ugliest face competitions are held annually in many English villages, but the most prestigious one is during the Egremont Crab Fair in the Lake District. In 1267, King Henry III granted the fair a Royal Charter, but gurning contests may not be as old as that.

For a **basic gurn** you jut your jaw forward then bring the bottom lip over the top one. Great gurners go further, covering the nose, too.

It helps to be toothless. Peter Jackman, a five-times winner of the competition, had all his teeth removed so he could perfect his gurn form.

Anne Woods, (above),
who was born in Egremont
(and died there in 2015),
won the ladies' competition
28 times in a row.
(Drawn from a photo by John Angerson/Rex.)

Defining "gurn"
A few possibilities:

- It could be just a mispronounced version of grin, possibly of Scottish origin…

- but in Northern Ireland, gurnin' means crying or whining.

- The *English Dialect Dictionary* says gurning is "to snarl as a dog; to look savage; to distort the countenance."

The Egremont event is not a crab fair; it's a crabapple fair. Crabapples are very bitter. If you ate one, you'd scrunch up your face too.

Contestants pull their faces while posing through a **horse halter.** This is called gurnin' through a braffin.

Welly Wanging
Throwing Wellington boots

Wang = throw
in Yorkshire

Upperthong,*
England
Late summer

The origin of this event followed an argument between two farmers in a pub. A pint of ale was spilled by one farmer into the welly of the other, who removed the boot, chased the the ale-spiller, and wanged his wet welly at him. No one can remember when this happened, or even if it's true.

*It's an unsubstantiated myth that locals shorten the village's name to Bra.

58

You can
throw the boot
any way you like:
one-handed, double-handed,
through the legs,
or backwards
(over the head),

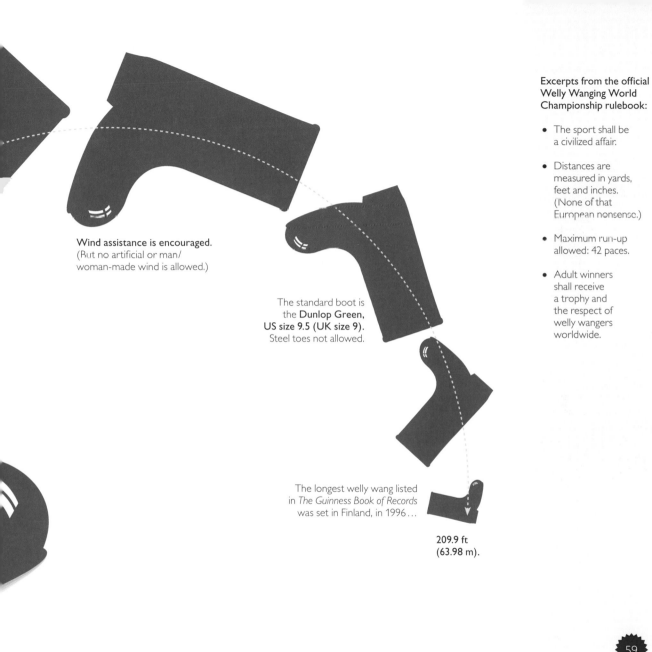

Wind assistance is encouraged.
(But no artificial or man/
woman-made wind is allowed.)

The standard boot is
the **Dunlop Green,
US size 9.5 (UK size 9).**
Steel toes not allowed.

The longest welly wang listed
in *The Guinness Book of Records*
was set in Finland, in 1996 …

**209.9 ft
(63.98 m).**

World
Worm
Charming
Championships

Willaston, England
Late June

Worm charming is a job in the US (to provide fishing bait), but the first real competition to coax worms from the ground just for fun was held in England in 1980, when Tom Shufflebotham persuaded 511 of them to show their shiny faces to the assembled, and astonished, crowd.

In the competition, teams typically consist of **a charmer** and **a catcher,** but there can be more.

Worms respond to **vibrations,** so that's what competitors concentrate on.

The charmer may use a variety of methods to produce vibrations that'll bring worms to the surface; for instance, poking the earth with a garden fork, banging sticks on the ground, playing bongo drums and recorders— even tap dancing on a platform over the area.

Naturally, **you can't just dig them up.**

Each team gets a **32 sq ft (3 sq m) plot** to work on.

The catcher watches for worms, but must be careful not to pull them up too soon. (Half worms don't count.)

The reason worms respond to charmers' vibrations is because they are similar to vibrations made by **moles,** which prey on worms.

But if they are going to be eaten by moles, wouldn't it be better if the worms wiggled **away** from the surface, not up through it?

Yes, I would have thought so.

Hmmm.

The world record is 567 worms retrieved in 2009 by 10-year-old Sophie Smith and her team in the 30-minute time allowed.

There's also a prize for heaviest worm.

Who's in charge here?

The competition's 18 rules were compiled and are enforced by The **International Federation of Charming Worms and Allied Pastimes** (IFCWAP). This regulatory body meets once a year.

Other charming events:

- **Devon Worm Charming**
  In May, annually since 1984, Blackawton, England. This one is mostly for children.

- **Canadian Worm Charming Championship and Festival**
  Annually in June, Shelburne, Ontario.

- **American Worm Gruntin' Festival**
  Annually since 2000, Sopchoppy, Florida.

  Gruntin' is what gathering worms for bait is called in the US.

61

World
Coal
Carrying
Championships

**Gawthorpe,
England**
Easter Monday

In 1963, Amos Clapham, a coal merchant, and a friend were having a drink in the Beehive Inn.* A third man came in and suggested that Amos looked under the weather. Whereupon Amos, who disagreed with the diagnosis, challenged the third man to a coal-carrying race to demonstrate that he was in fact perfectly fit.

*It seems that quite a few of the events in this book started out as a challenge in a pub.

① Bags of coal are lifted onto racers' shoulders.

② They **line up** on Owl Lane, outside the Royal Oak pub, and wait for the starter's pistol.

Men
carry a
110 lb (50 kg)
bag of coal.

Women
carry a
44 lb (20 kg)
bag of coal.

③ **They run,** with the bags on their shoulders.

The adult course (men and women) is about **0.6 mi (1 km).**

There's also a 500 ft (150 m) run for children (they don't carry coal, though).

The race **makes money for the upkeep of the village green** and its maypole.

As well as donations to the village, there are **trophies and cash prizes** in all categories of competition.

The trophy for the fastest time in the men's or veterans' races is this splendid object.

Runners must dump their bags opposite the Shoulder of Mutton pub, on Gawthorpe Village Green, near the maypole. **Finishing time is recorded when the bag of coal hits the green.**

Fastest time so far: just over **4 min.**

Race coaches are allowed, but they must stop at the Boot and Shoe pub. Only competitors are allowed to pass this point on the course.

4

5

Bog Snorkeling
Swimming in a peat bog

Llanwrtyd Wells, Wales
Last Monday in August

Bog Snorkeling started in 1976 in Llanwrtyd Wells (the smallest town in Britain, somewhere in the middle of Wales).

Flippers are allowed and wet suits are recommended, but some hardy (or foolish) souls swim in varying states of undress.

The races were
first called world
championships
in 1985.

Competitors must
swim **two lengths
of the 180 ft (55 m)**
peat bog without
using conventional
swimming strokes.

In 2014, the
fastest time
(1 min 23 sec)
was set by
a woman.

Llanwrtyd Wells
is also home to
the 22 mi (35.5 km)
Man vs. Horse Race.

Horses have
historically been
the winners.

Bog snorkeling also
takes place in **Australia,
Ireland, and Sweden,**
because there are
bogs there too.

World
Toe
Wrestling
Championship

England

**Fenny Bentley,
England**
June

In **1974**, four people in a pub invented a competition which the United Kingdom would always win (because no one else would know about it). For two years, an Englishman (one of the four inventors) did win, but as one story tells in **1976** a visiting Canadian took the toe trophy. With the whole point of the event now gone, it was discontinued.*

Toe wrestling is like arm wrestling, but with toes.

THE RULES

- **Shoes and socks are removed** by the opposing players.

- In preliminary rounds, **toes are inspected** by a qualified nurse, and cleared for competition.

- Since it often rains, competition takes place inside the **Bentley Brook Inn,** Fenny Bentley.

* Although the Olympic Committee has refused to recognize toe wrestling as a sport, **it has become popular again in recent years.**

THE EVENT

- **Two people compete in each "toedium."** ┈┈┈┈┈┐

- The bout starts when the umpire shouts, **"Toes away!"** Contestants lock toes and try to pin the other's foot to the side of the box for 3 sec.

- Each bout is the **best of three attempts.** First they lock right toes, then left toes, and finally the right toes again, if necessary.

The ultimate winner gets an **appropriately shaped trophy.**

- There are men's and women's championships, but no mixed matches.

- Top players have included Paul "Toeminator" Beech and Alan "Nasty" Nash.

BENTLEY BROOK INN

WORLD TOE WRESTLING CHAMPIONSHIPS

Hare Pie Scramble and Bottle Kicking

England

Hallaton and Medbourne, England
Easter Monday

There *is* a hare pie (or some other meat pie) and it is distributed to the villagers of Hallaton, who "scramble" to get a piece of it. However, there is no bottle, and it's not kicked.

Here's another misleadingly named English tradition with possible pagan origin.*

1

THE HARE
In the morning, the **ceremonial hare** (and the pie) are **paraded through the village of Hallaton.**

2

THE HARE PIE
Since 1770, a pie, some bread and beer have been provided to people in the village.**

3

SCRAMBLING THE PIE
When the procession reaches the church, **the pie is blessed** and **distributed to the crowd,** who try to catch a piece of it. Then the procession moves on to **Hare Pie Bank,** a nearby hill.

THE BOTTLES
They are actually 11 lb (5 kg) **barrels of beer.** ┈┈┈┈┈┈┈┈┈┈┈┈┈┈┈┈┈┈┈➤ Two of the barrels are
Three are used in the game. They are thrown up into the   filled with beer, while the
air above competing teams from Hallaton and **Medbourne**   third is solid wood and
(another village one mile away). Something like a rugby   is painted with stripes
scrum ensues between roughly 100 villagers.   of red, white, and blue.

KICKING THE BOTTLE
The point of the game is
for the participants from
the two villages to fight for
the barrel and **carry it
from Hare Pie Bank back
to their respective villages.**

It's the **best of three
barrels** and the struggle
can last for hours.

(But they don't
kick the barrels
or bottles
at all.)

*Pagan origin?
While the Hare Pie
and Bottle Kicking
festivities were first
recorded in 1770,
some think the
event started before
the Christian era, when
**hares were sacrificed
to the goddess Eostre.**

****Local lore fills out
the story: a hare
distracted a bull** who
was charging towards
two women from
Hallaton. They were
so grateful that they
gave money to the
local church, stipulating
that hare pie, bread,
and beer should be
provided for the villagers
every Easter Monday.
**One year, villagers from
Medbourne stole the
beer. A village rivalry
was born.**

World
Conker
Championships

England

**Southwick,
England**
2nd Sunday
in October

The first recorded
game of conkers
was in **1848**, but the
modern version
started in **1965**, after
a conversation in a
pub near Oundle
among a group
of frustrated fisher-
men whose trip
had been cancelled
because of rain.
Since **2009**, the
event has been held
in the Shuckburgh
Arms pub.

GETTING
READY

**Conkers and laces
are supplied**
to competitors.

Conkers are **used
only once.**

When children play the
game, they'll use many
different methods to
harden their favorites,
such as applying layers of
varnish, but nothing like
that is allowed at the
World Championships.
Oh no.

The lace (string) can
be wrapped round the
hand, but must hang
down **8 in (20 cm).**

Adjusting the knot
to make it bigger
is strictly forbidden.

PLAYTIME

 1 Each player has **nine strikes** at the opponent's conker. A coin is tossed to see who goes first.

2 **The first player gets the first three strikes.** Then the opponent has three attempts. They continue until each has had nine strikes, **unless**…

3 a conker is smashed. That ends the game.

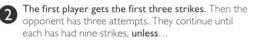

 4 If both conkers are smashed, there's a **replay.**

5 If a game takes more **than 5 min,** each player gets nine more strikes, alternating three to one player, three to the other.

6 If it's still not over, the player with **the most hits wins.**

 7 The ultimate winner, after everyone has played, is led to the **Conker Throne,** and crowned with conkers.

Throwing down the conker from above is probably the best way to smash the other player's conker, but some competitors swing from below, or round from the sides.

The only thing you can't do is deliberately tangle your lace (called **snagging**) around your opponent's. Do it three times and you are disqualified.

Conkers (in America they are called **buckeyes**) come from horsechestnut trees.

Conkers are known as **horse chestnuts** because they are fed to horses as a stimulant, and to make their coats shine.

One of the original fisherman in 1965 had a friend with vision problems, so it was decided at that very first meeting that any money raised by the event (and subsequent ones, if there were to be any) should go to charities for the **blind and vision-impaired.**

(Accompanying the championships there are **guide dog demonstrations,** as well as other attractions.)

World
Snail
Racing
Championship

Congham,
England
July

Held on Congham
village cricket field
since the 1960s,
the World Snail
Racing Championship
attracts some
400 avid amateur
malacologists (snail
experts) to the
often soggy event.
But then snails like
the damp, so it
doesn't matter if
it rains a bit.

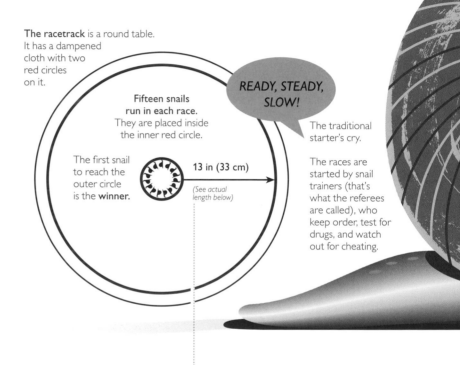

The racetrack is a round table.
It has a dampened
cloth with two
red circles
on it.

**Fifteen snails
run in each race.**
They are placed inside
the inner red circle.

The first snail
to reach the
outer circle
is the **winner**.

13 in (33 cm)

*(See actual
length below)*

*READY, STEADY,
SLOW!*

The traditional
starter's cry.

The races are
started by snail
trainers (that's
what the referees
are called), who
keep order, test for
drugs, and watch
out for cheating.

This is the actual distance that the snails run. ┄┄┄┄➤

72

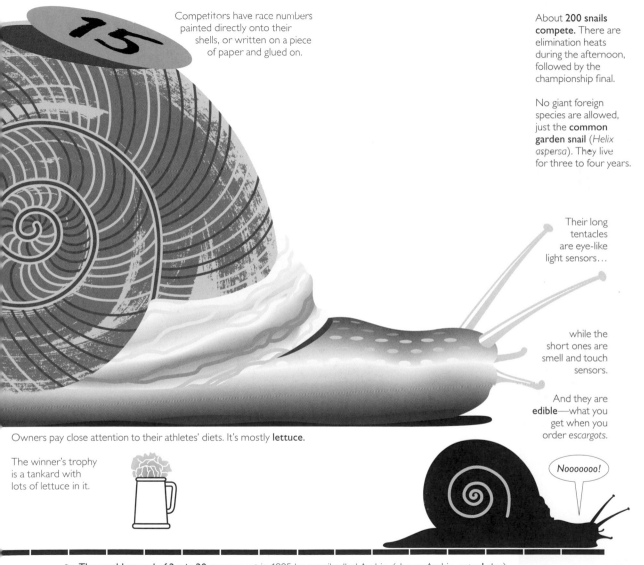

Competitors have race numbers painted directly onto their shells, or written on a piece of paper and glued on.

About **200 snails compete.** There are elimination heats during the afternoon, followed by the championship final.

No giant foreign species are allowed, just the **common garden snail** (*Helix aspersa*). They live for three to four years.

Their long tentacles are eye-like light sensors…

while the short ones are smell and touch sensors.

And they are **edible**—what you get when you order *escargots*.

Owners pay close attention to their athletes' diets. It's mostly **lettuce.**

The winner's trophy is a tankard with lots of lettuce in it.

Nooooooo!

--------> The **world record of 2 min 20 sec** was set in 1995 by a snail called Archie. (above: Archie, **actual size**)

Dwile Flonking*

England

Various villages
in Norfolk and
Suffolk, England
Summer

The first
documented game
of Dwile Flonking
was in 1966, at the
Beccles Festival
of Sport. The game's
earlier history
is muddled by a
(probably made-up)
story about a
document found
in an attic detailing
the rules. But who
cares? It's a lot of
silly, drunken fun, and
everyone disputes
the rules anyway.

*Dwile = piece of cloth
Flonking = either an
old term meaning flinging
or Old English ale

Two teams compete. The first team holds hands and dances in a circle around a member of the second team, who attempts to soak the dancers by flinging the beer-soaked dwile at them.

The circular dance is called **girting**. A full game comprises four **snurds**. (A snurd is one team taking a turn at girting.)

The man in the middle (the **flonker**) holds the **driveller** (a short hazel or yew stick). On the end of the driveller is the **dwile**. The flonker dips the dwile in the bucket of beer, then spins in the opposite direction to the dancers before flinging the dwile.

*Hmmmm…
I should paint
that.*

Matisse
senses an art
opportunity.

Scoring:

- **Three points:** a direct hit on a girter's head (called a **wanton**)

- **Two points:** a body hit (a **morther** or **marther**)

- **One point:** a leg hit (a **ripple** or **ripper**)

- If the dwile misses completely, it's called a **swadger** or **swadge**.

- When a swadger occurs, the flonker must drink ale from a **gazunder** (a chamber pot that "goes under" the bed), while the dancers chant **"pot, pot, pot."**

- **The team with the most points is declared the winner** after one point is deducted for any team member found to be sober at the end of the game.

World
Peashooting
Championships

**Witcham,
England**
2nd Saturday in July

In 1971,
John Tyson, the headmaster of Witcham village school, caught some students pinging each other with peashooters. This got him thinking that a peashooting competition might be a good way to raise money for the village hall.

Peashooters can be made of any material, but must be 12 in (30.4 cm) long.

The **peas** used are actually dried maple seeds, not garden peas, because peas have irregular shapes that get stuck in the shooter. All competition peas have a diameter of 0.25 in (5.5 mm).

In the first round, each person blows five of the officially sanctioned peas. The highest scorers go on to knockout blow-offs until a winner is declared.

Adults take aim **12 ft (4 m)** from the target.

Children aged seven and under take aim **8 ft (2.5 m)** from the target.
Ages 8 to 10 aim from 10 ft (3 m).

*It's worth bringing wellies just in case England lives up to the scurrilous rumor that it's always raining. (See also **Welly Wanging**, p 58.)

Some **peashooting equipment** is more than a simple tube. Around 2000, an avionics expert from nearby Lakenheath US Air Force base developed a **laser sight.** While they were horrified at first, village locals eventually embraced the idea.

(However, most competitors still use traditional peashooters, and they generally do just as well as their more technically advanced colleagues.)

76

Rolled straw bale

The target is lowered for children

Most of the competitors are locals, but the event also draws shooters from **Australia, New Zealand,** and the **US.**

Anyone of either sex or of any age may enter the Open Championship.

In addition, there are competitions just for women and children.

The target
is three rings of putty. Peas either stick to them or make dents, so it is easy to spot where they land. The closer to the center, the more points you get

5   3   1
points

12 in (30.4 cm)

Lawnmower Racing

Many places in England
May through October

Here's another sport dreamed up over a couple of beers! The year was 1973, the place was Wisborough Green, Sussex.

The British Lawnmower Racing Association (motto: *Per Herbam ad Astra,* "from grass to the stars") was set up to involve no sponsorship, no commercialization, no cash prizes, and no modification of the mowers' engines.

The BLMRA divides competing lawnmowers into **four groups,** and runs events for each.

GROUP 4
Wheel-driven, lawn tractor up to 18 hp, with an obvious bonnet over the engine

GROUP 3
Wheel-driven, garden ride-on, engine up to 18 hp, with no obvious bonnet

GROUP 2
Roller-driven, towed seat (it's steered with the feet)

GROUP 1
You run behind it (exhausting)

Top speed
How fast can you run?

Group 1 is not as popular as it used to be. The BLMRA hopes that racers will get up off their bums and run again. (Wearing a crash helmet is optional but it looks good.)

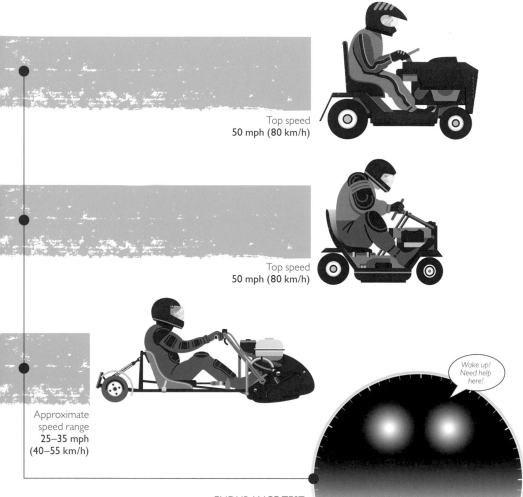

Top speed
50 mph (80 km/h)

Top speed
50 mph (80 km/h)

Approximate
speed range
**25–35 mph
(40–55 km/h)**

The BLMRA organizes a season of races all over the country at county shows, fairs and other events. **Points** are awarded to the first three finishers, and are added up as the season goes on (just like real motor racing). The champions are declared at the end of the season.

The Rules
Pretty strict. Anyone can enter, but mowers intended for racing in groups 4 and 3 must be **"homologated"** (inspected for eligibility in the group) and checked for general safety—for instance, **mowing blades must be removed.**

Racing abroad
In the past the BLMRA has raced in **France, Zimbabwe, Ireland, Luxembourg, Belgium, Finland,** and the **US.** There are regular races in **Luxembourg** and **Belgium,** and quite often a group from the UK will go.

Wake up! Need help here!

ENDURANCE TEST
The most grueling race in the competitive lawnmower year is held in August at Five Oaks, Billingshurst. It's a **12-hour event** in which drivers from groups 4, 3 and 2 complete as many laps of the course as they can from **8 pm to 8 am the next day.**

The pit crew is very important because **something inevitably breaks down.** (Lawnmowers are not built to mow, let alone *race*, for 12 hours non-stop!)

World
Poohsticks
Championships

Witney, England
June

In 1928, children's author A. A. Milne wrote about Pooh Bear's invention of the game Poohsticks in *The House at Pooh Corner*, his sequel to *Winnie-the-Pooh* (1926).

The first official version of the game was played in 1984 at Day's Lock on the River Thames, to raise money for charity. Since 2015, the championships have been held in Witney.

Any number of people can play wherever there's a river with a bridge over it, but at the **World Championships** there are **individual and team events**. Each player chooses a differently colored stick from the official pile.

 Players drop (not throw) their sticks into the river.

 The sticks go with the flow.*

*Probably no problem in England, but could become one if you play this game in Florida.

3 The players **rush to the other side of the bridge** to see which one emerges first.

4 **Blue** beats black in this round.

5 In an **alternate version** of Poohsticks, a marker is placed further down the river. The first stick to pass it is the winner.

③ ——→ ④ - - -→ ⑤ - - - - →

Shin Kicking
at the Cotswold Olimpicks

**Dover's Hill,
Chipping Campden,
England**
June

In 1612 Robert Dover started the Cotswold Olimpick Games (also known as Dover's Games). They continued until 1862, when they were stopped over a land dispute.

In 1951 the games were revived but were only held occasionally. A big boost in interest coincided with the official London Olympics in 2012.

Shin Kicking was one of the original competitions at the Cotswold Olimpicks, some 400 years ago. It's still the biggest draw at today's version of the games.

The referee is called a **stickler*** (look: he carries a long stick). When the stickler's stick is between two kickers, they must not kick.

THE RULES

- Competitors are provided with **white coats**, which represent traditional shepherds' smocks.
- Competitors must wear **long trousers**.
- **Padding the shins is allowed.** (Straw is provided.)
- Shoes can be **sneakers or boots with unreinforced toe caps.** Boots are checked.
- Partners in the first bouts are assigned **randomly**; winners go into the finals.
- Bouts begin with competitors holding each other's shoulders or lapels with straight arms.
- The stickler calls to stark kicking.
- **Throws** (or trips) must be preceded by a shin kick.
- **Winner is best of three throws** (or if "sufficient!" is called out by an opponent).

* It's believed that this is the origin of the English phrase, "a stickler for the rules."

Other games at the
Cotswold Olimpicks
include **Tug of War,
Throwing the Sledge-
hammer,** and **Spurning
the Barre.** (That last
one is similar to Tossing
the Caber, a Scottish
event in which huge
people throw a very
heavy, long wooden pole
as far as they can, making
it turn end-over-end.)

Cooper's Hill Wake
Cheese-rolling

England

Brockworth, England
Last Monday in May

Oh, those crazy English! They've been rolling wheels of cheese down Cooper's Hill in Brockworth since the 15th century.

(Some say it dates back to Roman times.)

Contestants line up at the top of the hill.

The official roller pushes the cheese down the hill a few seconds before the runners go.

The cheese used to be a wheel of Double Gloucester that weighed 9 lb (4 kg).

The real cheese sometimes veered off into spectators, so it was replaced by a lighter foam replica in 2013.

The hill is *really* steep; this part is not visible from the top.

As it rolls down the hill, the **cheese can reach 70 mph (112 km/h).**

Because of the danger—there have been injuries to both competitors and spectators —**the event was officially cancelled in 2010,** but it continues to be held, anyway, and roughly 4,000 people come to watch each year.

There are seven races:
- 1st Men's Downhill
- Boys 14 and Under Uphill
- 2nd Men's Downhill
- Girls 14 and Under Uphill
- Women's Downhill
- Mixed Open Uphill
- 3rd Men's Downhill

Anyone can enter, and there's no entry fee.

Double Gloucester cheese
The cheese wheel that used to be rolled is awarded to the winner. Since 1998 it has been handmade by Diana Smart, with milk from her Brown Swiss, Holstein and Gloucester cows. Diana is the only person still making the classic Double Gloucester cheese by hand. (Needless to say, it's delicious.)

What makes it "double?"
It is made with full cream **milk from both the morning and evening milkings.** A dye is added and it's aged for at least six months.

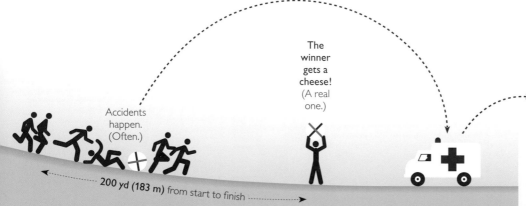

The winner gets a cheese! (A real one.)

Accidents happen. (Often.)

← 200 yd (183 m) from start to finish →

Danger!
Gloucestershire County Council posts warnings on roads leading to Cooper's Hill, to ensure everyone is aware of the potential dangers of attending and taking part.

Twelfth Night
Holly Man

London, England
Early January

Twelfth Night is celebrated around the world, but in England—always ready to add oddness to tradition—there's the Holly Man. He's rowed by volunteers along the River Thames in the Thames cutter *Trinity Tide* to Bankside, near Shakespeare's Globe Theatre.

The Holly Man (also called the **Green Man**, and seen on many English pub signs) is a character from pagan mythology. In winter, he wears holly and evergreens.

Together with London's **town crier**, the Holly Man toasts (or "wassails") the people, the river, and the theatre, to encourage growth.

*Usually the Twelfth Night is celebrated **12 days after Christmas** on January 5 or 6. This depends on the region, some start counting on the December 25, some on December 24. In London they are not very strict and celebrate at some day beginning of January.

At the end of the play **Twelfth Night Cakes** are given out. There's a **bean and a pea** hidden in two of the cakes, and the two lucky people who find them are crowned **King and Queen** for the day.

The King and Queen then lead the crowd in a procession through the streets to the **George Inn**, for storytelling, kissing the wishing tree, dancing, and drinking.

After the toasts, everyone moves to Bankside Jetty, where **mummers** (actors) perform a traditional play about St. George, patron saint of England.

Bognor Birdman
Humans try to fly

England

Bognor Regis,
England
September

In **1971**, a few enthusiastic fools tried to fly by jumping off the walkway leading to the Selsey lifeboat station on England's south coast. In 1978 the Birdman competitions moved to the pier in Bognor Regis, some 7 mi (10 km) east of Selsey, as part of Bognor's annual regatta.

There are **three classes** of competition:
- Kingfisher
- Leonardo da Vinci
- Condor

①

KINGFISHER CLASS
- Anything goes!
- Judged on topical or comic costume, a 2-min pre-flight "performance" on the pier, and crowd reaction.
- One helper is allowed on the pier deck.

A trophy is awarded for the **funniest moment,** and there are cash prizes for first, second and third in each class.

③

CONDOR CLASS
- Standard hang gliders
- Judged on **distance covered** and **longest time in the air.**
- Two helpers are allowed on the pier deck.
- Competitors get two attempts to fly, one on each day of the event.
- Condor-class flyers take off from the same platform as other classes, but only when the tide is lower, leaving 2 ft 6 in (0.75 m) of water for landing.

②

LEONARDO DA VINCI CLASS
- Self-designed and built aircraft; maximum wingspan 40 ft (12 m).
- Judged on **distance covered** and **longest time in the air.**
- Two helpers are allowed on the pier deck.
- Competitors get two attempts to fly, one on each day of the event.

A few rules:
- You must be **over 16.**
- You must be able to **swim 55 yd (50 m).**

Not allowed:
- kites
- balloons
- sailwings
- rockets
- cars
- catapults
- any "launch assistance from stored energy devices for propulsions"

89

World
Nettle-Eating
Championship

England

Marshwood,
England
June

Held at the
500-year-old
Bottle Inn
continuously since
2012—it started
in 1986 (see
opposite page)
but then the inn
closed for a few
years—this event
celebrates the
uncomfortable
practice of putting
lots of stinging
nettles into your
mouth and
swallowing them.

Stinging nettles are covered with
thousands of tiny, hollow tubes,
each one filled with a mixture
of toxic chemicals (including
three types of acid).

When the leaves touch skin,
the tubes snap and act like
microscopic needles that
pierce the skin and inject
the cocktail of nettle
venom into it.

The tongue and throat
become extremely irritated;
the mouth and lips turn black.

The taste of
nettles is a cross
between spinach and arugula.

1 Strip leaves off the stalk. Each one is 20 in (50 cm) long.

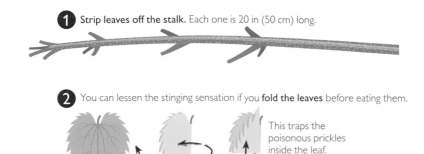

2 You can lessen the stinging sensation if you **fold the leaves** before eating them.

This traps the poisonous prickles inside the leaf.

3 Eat as many folded leaves as possible in **one hour. They must be the nettles provided.** No numbing agents are allowed, and no bathroom breaks.

4 Referees determine the winner by counting the **number of stalks** left next to each nettle-eater. Past winners have eaten the leaves from as many as 68 stalks.

The **story** about how it all started goes like this:

A farmer drinking in the Bottle Inn was boasting about the height of the nettles in some of his fields. They were **15.4 ft (4.7 m)** high. If anyone had bigger nettles, the farmer said he would eat his raw.

It wasn't long before another farmer brought in a **16 ft (4.8 m)** stalk.

The first farmer ate his nettles, and the tradition was born.

World
Beard and Mustache
Championships

Worldwide
Various locations
(but mostly in
Europe, so far)
Year-round

Despite claims
by Italy to have held
the first beard
competitions in
the 1970s, modern
bearding events
began in 1990 in
Germany. Since 1995,
international champi-
onships have been
held every two years.

The competition
is divided into three
main categories:

- Full beard
- Partial beard
- Mustache

Each category has precisely
defined sub-categories.

= no styling aids
(sprays or gels) permitted
during the competition

FULL BEARD

Natural

...with Styled Mustache

just the
mustache!

PARTIAL BEARD

Goatee Natural

Musketeer

Fu Manchu

MOUSTACHE

Natural

Dalí

English

92

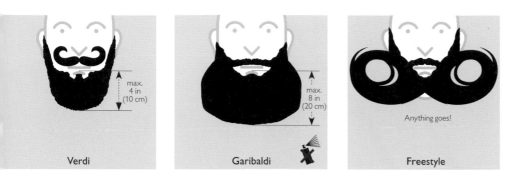

max. 4 in (10 cm)	max. 8 in (20 cm)	Anything goes!
Verdi	**Garibaldi**	**Freestyle**

	Hair grown only on cheeks and upper lip	Sideburns were introduced at the Carson City Championships in 2003 to honor Elvis Presley, but this is a controversial category.
Goatee Freestyle	**Imperial/Kaiser**	**Freestyle and Sideburns**

Anything goes!

Imperial **Hungarian** **Freestyle**

Some 300 men from 20 countries take part in the World Championships. The judges look beyond their facial hair, however wonderfully weird it might be, also taking into account the way participants dress to compliment their beards, and the poses they strike to best show off their facial creations.

Championship host cities:
1990 Höfen/Enz, Germany
1995 Pforzheim, Germany
1997 Trondheim, Norway
1999 Ystad, Sweden
2001 Schömberg, Germany
2003 Carson City, US
2005 Berlin, Germany
2007 Brighton, England
2009 Anchorage, US
2011 Trondheim, Norway
2013 Leinfelden, Germany
2015 Leogang, Austria
2017 Austin, US
2019 Antwerp, Belgium

No bearded ladies, yet. But the US Ladies' Fake Beard and Mustache Society does organize the **Whiskerinas Competition.** It happens at the same time as the men's national events. (The fake beards don't all have to be hair!)

El Entroido de Laza
A carnival with fire ants

Laza, Spain
February/March

The origin of throwing fire ants in Laza is unclear, but there's a story of a judge who didn't like the carnival, and would not give an employee time off for the fun. So friends teamed up with the worker and threw bags of fire ants at the grumpy judge.

The word *entroido* comes from the Latin *introitus*, meaning **entrance**. In this case, "entrance" refers to a **beginning**—of spring, or Lent, when many towns in Galicia (and elsewhere, of course) hold carnivals.

El Entroido de Laza includes **parades, odd characters,** and **feasting** for five days leading up to Ash Wednesday.

On **Sunday**, teams of up to 40 masked *peliqueiros* run through the streets. Spectators are not allowed to touch them or call their names because for that one day they have spiritual authority.

On **Monday**, there's a friendly battle amongst locals who throw **flour, ash,** and finally **balls of mud** filled with **fire ants** that have been agitated with vinegar to make them especially angry.

The battle lasts about 20 min. Then everyone goes off, white-faced (and possibly stinging), for a drink.

94

While Laza's carnival has fire ants, **other towns in Galicia** have special events during their own *entroidos*.

Among them: **Viana do Bolo, Ourense,** where masked *boteiros* parade to very loud bands then eat a local stew at the Festa da Androlla.

Cobres, Pontevedra, the version of **El Entroido** that is most geared towards younger people, with special events for children and teens.

Verin, Ourense, a parade of masked *cigarróns*, who represent ancient tax collectors.

Xinzo de Limia, Ourense, where *pantallas* wearing distinctive masks (as in all the villages at El Entroido) take control of the streets for a day.

How an ant gets you: first, it anchors its mandibles on the prey (during the carnival that could be you). (See the other end of the drawing; mandibles are like jaws.)

Then the ant's **stinger** delivers **venom** from a **sac** to your skin, causing an intense burning sensation.

The *peliqueiros* are all young men, but they wear women's stockings, puffy shorts and a belt with clanging cowbells. To scare evil away, they carry a **whip.**

A model of a giant fire ant appears in the centre of Laza during El Entroido; this drawing shows the comparative sizes of the model and a real *peliqueiro*.

And here's a fire ant, actual size.

Spain

Danza de los Zancos
Stilt dancing

Anguiano, Spain
Several times a year
(one event during Mary
Magdalene festival in July)

In honor of the local saint, Mary Magdalene,
eight young men from the oldest families
in this small town whirl down cobbled streets
on wooden stilts (zancos). No one seems to
know the origin of the stilt dances. But they
are fun to watch.

The first reference to the Danza de los
Zancos was in **1603**. The tradition has
been passed from father to
son ever since.

It looks dangerous (it is
dangerous), but dancers
seldom fall; they enter a
sort of trance-like state, and
stare straight ahead to keep
their balance, and to help them
keep out of the way of the crowds
lining the narrow streets

Their soft skirts billow out to **this shape**
when the dancers start spinning, and they
clack castanets as they go. One of the
steep hills they descend is named after
them: the **Cuesta de los danzadores.**

The **action starts** in Anguiano's main church, where dancers pick up a small icon of the Magdalena (Mary Magdalene). Then they "dance" with her down the cobbled streets to a specially created shrine. The icon stays there until the last Saturday of September, when it's taken back to the church for the winter.

Stilt walking is also part of religious festivals in **Central Africa, Ecuador, France, and Puerto Rico.**

97

La Batalla del Vino

Haro, Spain
June 29

In the 13th century, the town of Haro had a border dispute with its neighbor Miranda de Ebro. Haro marked its borders with crimson flags every Saint Peter's Day. Over time, this tradition became a fiesta with lots of wine consumed (and spilled), and was officially called the Battle of Wine in 1965.

Haro is known as the capital of the Rioja wine region. There are **four categories** of Rioja red wine:

Rioja	less than a year old (in an oak aging barrel)
Crianza	two years old (one of them in an oak aging barrel)
Rioja Riserva	three years old (one of them in an oak aging barrel)
Rioja Gran Riserva	five years old (two years in oak, three years in bottle)

The most widely used grape is **Tempranillo,** but Rioja red wines are typically a blend of various grapes.

WHAT HAPPENS

1 It all starts in the morning at **7 am,** with a **procession** through the town.

2 Everyone wears **white shirts and red scarves.** They carry *botas* (boots), bottles, buckets and water guns filled with **red wine.**

3 They are led by the **Mayor of Haro** to the cliffs of Bilibio where a **mass** is celebrated.

About **13,200 gal (50,000 L) of Riojan wine is thrown in the morning of June 29.** (That's enough to fill roughly 300 standard bath tubs.)

 4

After mass, **everyone pours wine over each other.** The shirts aren't white any more.

 5

At noon, everyone goes back to the **Plaza de la Paz in Haro.** Here the wine is drunk, instead of being thrown.

6

In the evening, there are **"bullfights."** They are fought between young men (who by that time are pretty drunk) and young female cows—heifers. It's mostly just fun with no human or animal deaths.

San Fermín Festival
The running of the bulls

Spain

Pamplona, Spain
Eight-day event, starting
annually on July 7

The route is
900 yd (825 m)
and the run takes
about 3 min,
starting at 8 am
on each day
of the festival.

Runners say this
prayer before
setting off:
"We beseech
San Fermin to
guide us in this
run and to give
us his blessing."

The festival started in the 13th century.
(San Fermin is the patron saint of Pamplona.)
It's a mix of **logistics** and **fun.**

Logistics: moving bulls from temporary corrals at one end of the town
to the bullring at the other for the evening's fights.

Fun: running in front of the bulls as they gallop through
Pamplona's narrow streets (if you think that's fun).

Six fighting bulls (and some smaller bullocks) run each day. The big bulls weigh about 1,545 lb (700 kg), which is a lot to have breathing down your neck.

The bulls follow about 2,000 people who run each day of the festival.

If you want to run, there are rules:

- You must be over 18.
- You must not be drunk.
- You must wear the official attire:

red handkerchief* tied round your neck;

white shirt;

long red scarf* tied round your waist;

white trousers.

*Can be easily and cheaply bought at the festival.

The most dangerous part of the run is not so much the bulls themselves— it's other runners tripping up in front of you.

So beware: since 1924, 15 people have died and 200 have been injured as a result of goring. New runners are advised not to run on the first day. Watch what you're in for first!

El Colacho
Jumping over babies

Burgos

Spain

Castillo de Murcia, Spain
Annually in June, on the first Sunday after the Catholic Feast of Corpus Christi

El Salto de Colacho (the devil's jump) dates back to the 1620s. The idea is to cleanse the babies' original sin and offer them lifelong protection against illness.

Babies aged up to one year old (usually four or six of them, in two rows) lie on a series of mattresses placed in the middle of the street. Then the *colachos* run down the street **leaping over them.**

102

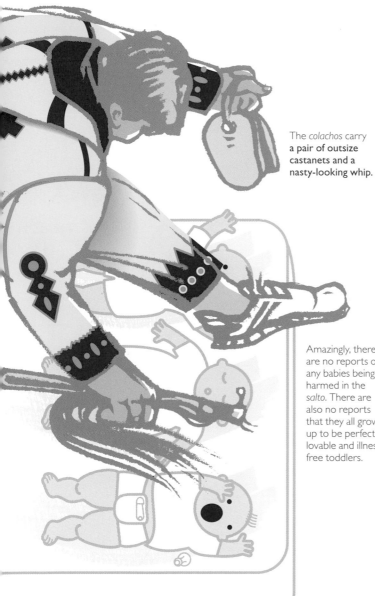

The *colachos* carry **a pair of outsize castanets and a nasty-looking whip.**

Amazingly, there are no reports of any babies being harmed in the *salto*. There are also no reports that they all grow up to be perfectly lovable and illness-free toddlers.

The Catholic Church maintains that **baptism (by water) is the proper way to rid an infant of original sin**, rather than a jumping devil. **The church would like to see El Colacho ended.**

If your mother didn't put your life in danger as a one-year-old, and you weren't "jumped," don't worry, you can take part in Las Hogueras de San Juan — the bonfires of St. John — held every June 23 (St. John's Eve). Children and teenagers jump over the remains of fires lit on Postiguet Beach, Alicante, as well as all over Spain.

Jarramplas
Turnip-Throwing Festival

Piornal, Spain
January 19 and 20
(San Sebastián Day)

Although any religious or other origins are unknown,* the Jarramplas Festival has been imbued with deep meaning by the people of Piornal: it's the triumph of good over evil, by means of flying turnips aimed at a devil in fancy dress.

*The simplest theory: the punishment of a notorious cattle thief.

The men of Piornal wait **for years** to play the part of the Jarramplas. And when it's their turn, they dress up like this.

Spain

While being pelted, the Jarramplas **beats his drum** and taunts the crowd.

15,000 huge and hard turnips are trucked into Piornal. Local businesses board up their windows.

The mask and costume hide extensive **armor and padding,** which are needed to protect the wearer from the cascade of turnips from locals (and from tourists; but if you go be prepared to be bruised by badly aimed vegetables).

As well as an **upper body metal breast-plate,** the Jarramplas wears **padded metal tubes** to protect his legs. The mask is strapped onto the breastplate.

The festival starts at noon on January 19, with a **religious service** dedicated to San Sebastián. After this, a statue of the saint is paraded through the streets, followed by the pelting of the unfortunate Jarramplas.

The turnip onslaught goes on for as long as the **Jarramplas can stand it** before retiring to the church that he started from. He then appears outside the church without his mask and is **applauded by the crowd.**

Another Jarramplas emerges and is immediately assaulted. The whole thing **continues for two days.** The Jarramplas **who lasts longest is honored in the town.**

105

Fiesta del Orgullo Gay
High heels race

Madrid, Spain
June/July

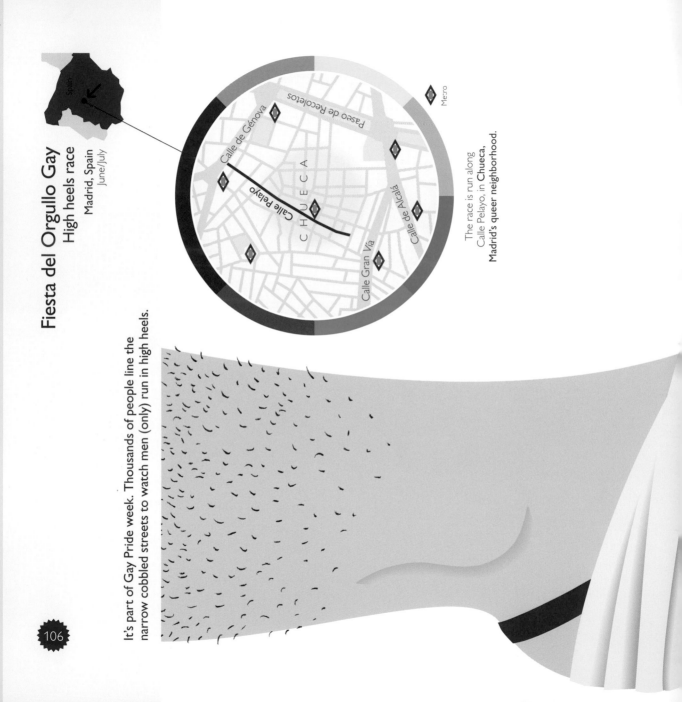

Calle de Génova

Paseo de Recoletos

Metro

CHUECA

Calle Pelayo

Calle Gran Vía

Calle de Alcalá

The race is run along
Calle Pelayo, in **Chueca**,
Madrid's queer neighborhood.

It's part of Gay Pride week. Thousands of people line the narrow cobbled streets to watch men (only) run in high heels.

Runners strap
their shoes on
tightly with
packing tape.

This shoe is **actual size.**
A message to all: see what
it looks like next to your foot.
Then think about the agony that
the women (or other men)
in your life put up with
to fulfil your (or their)
fantasies.

**For the
race, heels
must be
5.9 in
(15 cm) high.**

They are
scrupulously
measured
before
the start.

**It's fitting that men
are elevating themselves (again).**
When high heels were introduced
as a fashion statement in the early
1600s, **men were the first** to wear
them. Heels were a sign of power
and privilege.

It wasn't until the 1730s that women
started to wear high heels.

Els Enfarinats
A flour and egg battle

Ibi, Spain
December 28

This takes place on El Día de los Inocentes (Day of the Innocents). It's Spain's equivalent of April Fool's Day, and indeed it's full of fun (and flour, eggs, firecrackers, and fire extinguishers).

Els Enfarinats was started in 1981 when Ibi restored a 200-year-old tradition; the origin is thought to have grown from the Fiesta de los Locos (Feast of Fools) that was part of the Roman festival of Saturnalia.

A **mock coup d'état** between **two groups** is fought in mock military dress.

- **Els Enfarinats** (literally "the floured ones") are married men who take over the village of Ibi, starting at **8 am.**

- At **9 am** a new mayor of **Els Enfarinats** is decided.

- Under the slogan "New Justice," **silly laws made up on the day are imposed** by the temporary dictatorship, and people who infringe them **are fined.**

- (All money collected goes to local charities.)

- People who refuse to pay are sent to mock jails set up in the street.

Hundreds of pounds of flour and more than **1,500 eggs** are thrown in the annual battle.

- **The second group is La Oposició,** who try to restore order.

- **Flour** is liberally thrown, and people **gradually become invisible** in the white haze.

- At 5 pm the authority of Els Enfarinats ends, and everyone goes off for a traditional *dansá* (a festive ball).

Cascamorras
Returning the Virgin

Spain

Guadix and Baza, Spain
September

More than 500 years ago, a worker (nicknamed Cascamorras) from the village of Guadix, was building a church in the village of Baza and found a statue of the Virgen de la Piedad (Our Lady of Mercy) buried in the ground. He attempted to bring the image back to Guadix, but was foiled by the villagers of Baza.

A court allowed Baza to keep the statue, but said that Guadix could celebrate the day with a festival, and during the festivities if anyone from Guadix could get the statue back without being daubed in oil, they could keep it. So every year, Cascamorras tries and gets very dirty!

The festival consists of two "runs":

September 6 **THE BAZA RUN**
(In which Cascamorras tries to bring the statue back to Guadix.)

Each year, Guadix chooses **a young man to play the role of Cascamorras.** He wears a traditional clown-like outfit and carries a big flag with an image of the Virgin. He also has a *porro* (a rubber ball, or a bladder tied to a stick with a leather strap), which he uses to fend off people who want to make him dirty.

Cascamorras doesn't run all the way from Guadix to Baza—about 24 mi (39 km). Instead, **he travels to Baza the night before his run through the town.**

Because Cascamorras returns home empty-handed, the locals in Guadix are "angry," and give him a welcome similar to the one he got in Baza, but this time they **daub him with ochre and blue paint.**

Villagers from Baza cover themselves in black oil. When Cascamorras runs through the village, they rub against him and spray oil over him so he doesn't reach the Convent of Mercy (and the statue of the Virgin) unstained.

After the run, Cascamorras, his backup team, and the oil-soaked villagers are permitted to **enter the convent** to bathe and clean up the mess.

If you go, prepare to get dirty, and wet: people lean over their balconies in houses lining the route in Guadix and empty buckets of water onto the crowd below, and the fire brigade cools everyone off with hoses.

2

September 9
THE GUADIX RUN
(In which Cascamorras returns to Guadix without the statue.)

Once again, he doesn't run all the way between the two villages.

La Tomatina
Throwing tomatoes

Spain

Buñol, Spain
Last Wednesday
in August

Started in 1945,
La Tomatina
was banned twice
in the '50s, but is
now one of Spain's
most popular
festivals.

Goggles
and gloves,
are recommended.

It all gets going at **10 am** when youths climb up the *palo jabón*—a greased pole with a lump of pork at the top. Once the pork has been dislodged, the fight itself starts.

Tomato-filled trucks drive into the main square, and the crowd are pelted with 150,000 tomatoes signaling the start of a one-hour food fight.

You are supposed to crush the tomatoes before hurling them.

Tomatoes are specially grown for the event in Extremadura (where they're cheaper and less tasty).

Afterwards, the streets are hosed down; it's said that the acidity of the tomatoes leaves them perfectly clean.

Some other countries that hold Tomatina-like events: Chile, China, Colombia, Costa Rica and India, as well as five cities in the US.

113

La Batalla de Ratas
Throwing dead rats

Spain

El Puig, Spain
Last Sunday in January

In a centuries-old celebration of San Pedro Nolasco's saint's day, people in El Puig smash *cucañas* (like *piñatas*, but made of clay). Half of them are filled with dead rats, the rest with candy.

When the rats fall out, they are thrown back and forth within the crowd, to the disgust (or delight) of all.

In 1237, when the festival started, the *cucañas* were filled with fresh fruit and nuts—tasty treats for live rats, who managed to get inside. Smashing the *cucañas* released them, still alive but dazed. (Today, they use frozen rats, which are more hygienic.)

The whole thing was banned in 2012, but the people of El Puig still continue the old tradition despite the ban.

Long live dead rats!

115

Concurs de Castells de Tarragona
Human tower competition
Tarragona, Catalonia, Spain
Biennially in September/October

In 2010, *castell* (castle) building became part of UNESCO's Masterpieces of Oral and Intangible Heritage of Humanity.

Spain

The *enxaneta* —traditionally a lightweight boy or girl—climbs to the top of the *pom de dalt*, or tower dome, and stays there for just a few seconds, raising an arm to salute the crowds with four fingers outstretched, reflecting the stripes of the Catalan flag.

The kids often wear foam-padded helmets.

The tower (*tronc*) consists of up to five people in the lower rings, reducing to two just below the top. Ten levels is about the limit.

Deconstructing the tower without it falling apart is difficult. Teams practice this procedure as much as they do building it.

There are many variations on the construction of the towers; in one, a multi-level column of one person standing on the shoulders of another is built *inside* the kind of tower shown here.

Throughout Catalonia, teams of *colles castelleres* compete to construct elaborate versions of the human towers that were first built in 1712 in Valls, near Tarragona.

Castellers traditionally wear white trousers, a bandana and a colored shirt, denoting the team (**Castellers de Barcelona** wear red). But the most important part of the clothing is the **sash** (*faixa*). This supports the lower back, and is also a foothold for other team members when they climb up the tower.

Most *castellers* go barefoot to stop them injuring colleagues' shoulders.

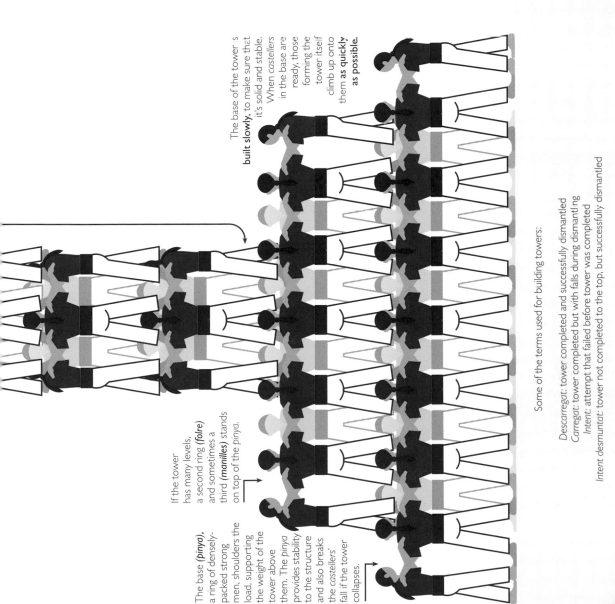

The base of the tower is **built slowly**, to make sure that it's solid and stable. When *castellers* in the base are ready, those forming the tower itself climb up onto them **as quickly as possible.**

If the tower has many levels, a second ring (*folre*) and sometimes a third (*manilles*) stands on top of the *pinya*.

The base (*pinya*), a ring of densely-packed strong men, shoulders the load, supporting the weight of the tower above them. The *pinya* provides stability to the structure and also breaks the *castellers*' fall if the tower collapses.

Some of the terms used for building towers:

Descarregat: tower completed and successfully dismantled
Carregat: tower completed but with falls during dismantling
Intent: attempt that failed before tower was completed
Intent desmuntat: tower not completed to the top, but successfully dismantled

Fierljeppen
Canal jumping

Netherlands

Belgium
Germany

**Throughout
the Netherlands**
May through September
(The Dutch National
Championship is held
at the end of August.)

**The first official
competition was
held in 1771
(written records
go back to 1200),
but canal jumping
wasn't structured
as a sport until
1957. By 1966
there were two
leagues, and the
championship
started in 1972.**

About a quarter of the Netherlands
is reclaimed land that's below sea
level, and it's kept from flooding by
a **grid of drainage channels**. Farmers found
it was more efficient to jump over these
channels than to walk to the nearest
bridge. In the 20th century, this became
a sport. Unlike Olympic pole vaulting,
the object is length, not height.

Competitors have
2 min to **plant their
pole** (in the canal)…
then they **sprint**
along a 66 ft (20 m)
runway,…

1

they **leap** onto
the pole,…

2

Jumpers
often pull
bicycle **inner
tubes** over
one ankle for a
better grip.

and
shimmy
up as far
as they
can
while
keeping
the pole
upright.

3

The pole has a disc
at its base to stop
it from sinking into
the canal bed.

It's not as easy as you might think! Jumpers must control the pole's direction as it bends forward; the **key to a long jump** is knowing when to let go and fling the body into the sandpit.

This kind of pole vaulting takes place in **other parts of the world** (US, Japan), where jumpers are more likely to end up in the water than in a sandpit. The Netherlands is the only country where it's taken seriously as a sport rather than entertainment.

Historically wooden, today's **poles** are usually made of carbon fiber or aluminum. A good-quality one costs about EUR 300. Maximum length is 43 ft (13 m).

Each competitor gets three jumps.

Roughly a third of vaulters get wet. (The crowd loves that.)

Sandpit

The longest jump recorded is 70.5 ft (21.5 m), but amateurs can easily do half that.

There's a theory that **Henry VIII** of England fell on his head while pole-vaulting over a brook, and that this accident (together with two jousting injuries) led to his erratic behaviour (for instance, chopping off two of his wives' heads).

Amsterdam
Cannabis Cup

Belgium | Netherlands | Germany

Amsterdam,
Netherlands
November

The original
competition and
celebration was
founded in **1987**
by **Steven Hager,**
an **American**
advocate for the
legalization of
marijuana. It was
subsequently named
the **High Times
Cannabis Cup.**
In **2015,** the
Amsterdam event
was taken over by
Dutch enthusiasts.

In the competition, **different types
of marijuana** are judged and trophies
are awarded in many categories,
including best edibles and highest level
of CBD in cannabis products. (CBD is
cannabidiol, one of at least 110 active
medical components in cannabis.)

Awards also go to best booth
and other cannabis-related
products in the accomp-
anying trade show.

The two basic types of weed:

Sativa (*Cannabis sativa*) is a tall plant, reaching
about 19 ft (6 m), with narrow leaflets, separated
branches, and spear-like flower clusters.
Primarily affects the mind and emotions.

Benefits include:
- reduces depression
- relieves headaches and migraine
- energizes and stimulates
- increases focus and creativity
- stimulates appetite.

Indica (*Cannabis indica*) is a short, bushy plant, about
5 ft (1.5 m) high, with broad, overlapping leaflets, and denser
flower buds than Sativa. **Primarily affects the body.**

Benefits include:
- reduces pain and inflammation
- reduces pressure inside eyes
- relaxes muscles
- assists sleep
- reduces nausea
- stimulates appetite.

In 1997, **the Counter-culture Hall of Fame** was created to celebrate the history of cannabis counterculture and the people who have shaped it.

Members included:

- **Bob Marley** (1997)
- **Louis Armstrong** (1998)
- **William Burroughs, Allen Ginsberg, Jack Kerouac,** (1999)
- **Bob Dylan** (2002)
- **Tommy Chong, Cheech Marin** (2007)
- **Peter Tosh** (2008)
- **Alexander Shulgin, Ann Shulgin** (2014)

Alexander Shulgin was an American chemist and psycho-pharmacologist. In the 1970s, he introduced MDMA (ecstasy) to the field of psychology. With his wife Ann, he wrote *PIHKAL. A Chemical Love Story* and *TIHKAL. The Continuation,* which described the couple's work with these two psychoactive drugs.

Want to go?
Anyone can attend the Amsterdam Cannabis Cup. **(there's no age limit),** and package tours are available. Tickets include entrance to the Cup events, the trade show, and music events. And...there are some **200 cannabis coffeeshops in Amsterdam.**

In 2010, the first High Times Cannabis Cup in the **US** took place in San Francisco, followed later by Colorado, Michigan, Oregon, Southern California, and Washington.

In 2015, a Cannabis Cup was held in **Negril, Jamaica.** It is planned to make it an annual event there.

121

Watt-olümpiade
Mud Olympics

Denmark
Germany
France

**Brunsbüttel,
Germany**
July

The German Mud Olympics were started in 2004. Today, teams from 46 countries compete in football, volleyball, handball, and a kind of sledge racing.

This event, like the Korean Mud Festival (opposite page), celebrates getting very dirty while keeping a sense of humor (and raising lots of money for charity).

122

◄┈┈ The Wattolümpiade takes place on natural mudflats.

The Boryeong Mud Festival takes place in plastic inflatable pools.

Boryeong Mud Festival

Daecheon Beach, Boryeong, South Korea
July

Since 1998, a muddy wonderland has been set up on Daecheon Beach: 200 US t (180 t) of smooth, gray dirt is hauled in from nearby mud-flats, and dumped into huge man-made pools. Brave people wrestle, slide and get dirty. Then they shower, or jump in the sea. Less brave folk can have mud massages, or get their bodies painted with colored mud.

The festival started as a marketing gimmick for Boryeong mud cosmetics, which are full of minerals, bentonites and germanium.

If **"Where there's mud, there's fun"** isn't an old saying, it should be.

123

Battaglia delle Arance
Orange battle

Ivrea, Italy
During Carnevale,
February/March

The annual recreation of a centuries-old fight between the starving people of Ivrea and their tyrannical ruler.

Around 1200 BCE, **the evil baron of Ivrea** was overthrown when **Violetta**, a miller's daughter who was about to be married, rebelled against the tyrant's rule that he was allowed to bed every young bride.

Violetta did go to the tyrant's castle but then **beheaded** him, inciting the townspeople to revolt.

While he was alive, the baron had twice yearly given **beans** to the poor, who threw them into the street as a sign of contempt.

In the 19th century, beans were replaced by **oranges** at carnival time.

After World War II, the simple act of throwing oranges at the parade turned into a friendly **battle between orange-throwers (*aranceri*) representing the people and more throwers representing the evil baron.**

For the people:
4,000 *aranceri* on foot, divided into nine teams, wearing distinctive team colors.

Beware of flying oranges: the city of Ivrea provides 500 US t (500 t) of them for the event.

124

Why oranges?
Three theories:

- They symbolize the head of the despised tyrant.
- They symbolize the removed testicles of the despised tyrant.
- In 19th-century Italy, they were the most exotic thing that girls could throw at boys in the parade whom they wanted to court.

Representing the baron's army:
50 horse-drawn carts, with 10 or 12 *aranceri* in each one. They wear protective clothing and masks that mimic 11th-century armor.

Every year, a young woman is chosen to be the defiant Violetta in the parade. She wears a red headscarf, and if you are among the 100,000 spectators, you should wear a red hat too. It *might* stop you from being targeted by orange-throwers.

Calcio Storico Fiorentino
Ball and fights

Florence, Italy
June 24
(Feast Day of
St. John the Baptist,
Florence's patron saint)

The rules
of this brutal
event were first
published in 1580 by
Giovanni de' Bardi,
a Florentine count.

Calcio means kick in
Italian, and there's
plenty of kicking
involved, as well as
punching and wres-
tling, head-butting,
elbowing and choking,
all mixed up with
elements of football
and rugby.

In the 16th century, **the game was played exclusively by aristocrats,** every night between Epiphany (the 12th day after Christmas) and Lent.

Today, **four teams,** representing the historical neighborhoods of the city, play against each other in the first round, then the winners of those two games meet in the final on July 24.

Each team has 27 players.

Blue: Santa Croce
White: Santo Spirito
Red: Santa Maria Novella
Green: San Giovanni

1 **At the start** of the game, following the referee's throw-in, the team that gets possession of the ball casually passes it back and forth between team members…

2 while their **front line** of fighters punch, kick, and wrestle with the opposing team, trying to stop them moving forward.

Players
wear traditional
baggy pants in their
team's colors.

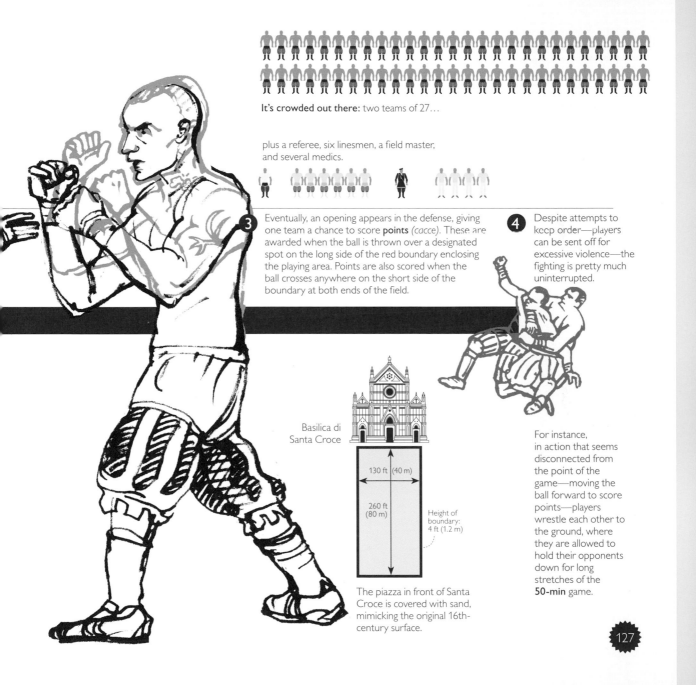

It's crowded out there: two teams of 27…

plus a referee, six linesmen, a field master, and several medics.

3 Eventually, an opening appears in the defense, giving one team a chance to score **points** *(cacce)*. These are awarded when the ball is thrown over a designated spot on the long side of the red boundary enclosing the playing area. Points are also scored when the ball crosses anywhere on the short side of the boundary at both ends of the field.

4 Despite attempts to keep order—players can be sent off for excessive violence—the fighting is pretty much uninterrupted.

Basilica di Santa Croce

130 ft (40 m)

260 ft (80 m)

Height of boundary: 4 ft (1.2 m)

The piazza in front of Santa Croce is covered with sand, mimicking the original 16th-century surface.

For instance, in action that seems disconnected from the point of the game—moving the ball forward to score points—players wrestle each other to the ground, where they are allowed to hold their opponents down for long stretches of the **50-min** game.

127

Il Palio di Siena
Horse race

Siena, Italy
July 2 and August 16

10 horses and their riders take part in this famous race, first run in 1656. It's fast and dangerous—most years, some horses cross the finish line without their riders.

Before the main event, there's a two-hour parade (Corteo Storico) round the track. The race itself lasts about 90 sec.

The Palio is known for corrupt deals and, forsaking the glory of winning, many jockeys take money for deliberately losing.

The Piazza del Campo
The festival lasts four days; preparations take the whole year.

Temporary stands ( ) are installed for spectators. Seats are expensive and usually sell out well in advance.

Spectators (•••••••) can also watch from **balconies** on the buildings surrounding the piazza (they can be rented for the festival).

San Martino bend

Direction of the race

Start and **finish** line

Del Casato bend

A loud **cannon-like blast** signals the start of the race and, after **three laps,** four blasts mark the end.

The central area of the piazza is free to the public, who arrive early in the morning through **this entrance.** They have a long wait—the Corteo Storico pageant starts at 5 pm, and the Palio starts at 7.30 pm (the July race), and 7 pm (the August race).

Jockeys wear the **distinctive colours** of their district.

Anything goes
Riders grab and shove other horses and jockeys. Whips are used on other horses as well as their own.

Purebreds are not allowed; all the horses are of **mixed breed**.

The horses are ridden **bareback.** Even good riders are easily thrown off.

Before race day, the city lays down **several inches of clay and sand** over the piazza's stone surface. This provides a certain amount of grip for the horses' hooves.

The Palio is as much about ongoing rivalries between the *contrade* (city wards) as it is about the fastest horse. (And among members of a *contrada*, the loser is the one that finishes second, not last.)

There are 17 city wards in **Siena.** In 1729, the city's governor stipulated that in the interests of safety, only **10 of the 17** *contrade* could take part during each of the two annual races. (The seven that do not run take part in that month's race the following year. Another three, chosen by draw, make up the total.)

The first horse to cross the finish line wins, even if riderless.

The winner is awarded a silk banner *(palio),* hand-painted by a different artist for each race.

Krampuslauf
The Krampus Run

Klagenfurt, Austria
During the weeks leading up to December 6 (Feast of St. Nicholas)

Krampus is half-goat, half-demon. During the Krampus Run an estimated 1,000 of them parade loudly and drunkenly through the streets of Klagenfurt.

Krampus is the dark companion of **Saint Nicholas** (**St. Nick, or Santa Claus**). While St. Nick rewards children with toys, Krampus punishes misbehaving children by beating them with birch twigs, and then **carries them off in his sack** so he can eat them later.

(And don't they just look delicious? Mmmm!)

Where the **Krampus legend** comes from is not clear, but he may have been a pre-Christian pagan spirit, whom the Catholic Church later transformed into the **devil**. Or he may just have been the devil who escaped from hell, and that's why he **carries rusty chains.**

Krampus rattles **the chains** to instill fear in children as he runs through Klagenfurt.

In addition to Austria, there are **Christmas pageants** that feature both Santa Claus and Krampus in **Germany** (Bavaria), **Italy**, **Slovenia**, **Croatia**, and **Hungary**. But **Austria** has by far the biggest Krampus celebrations. (It seems that children would be advised to behave well in Austria!)

There's even a **Krampus Museum** in Suetschach, about 14 mi (23 km) from Klagenfurt.

The **female version** of Krampus is **Perchta**, a pagan goddess, and there's usually a **Perchtenlauf** (Perchta Run) at the same time as the Krampuslauf.

The **mask** worn by Perchta makes her just as scary as her male equivalent. (Perhaps, as a woman, she is believed to be the one who knows the most about how naughty children can be.)

Busójárás*
Scaring away Ottoman troops

Mohács, Hungary
The week before Ash Wednesday

In 1526, the Croatian minority living in Mohács dressed in horned masks and, making as much noise as they could, drove away the invading Ottoman army. Now it's an annual celebration held at the end of the carnival season.

*In Hungarian the name means "buso walking." The masked characters are Busó.

Each Busó has his own **unique carved wooden mask.**

Today, there are a few female Busós, but it's more usual for women to dress as Ottoman Turks— **the enemy!**

The **noisemaker** is essential!

As well as his mask, the Busó wears a **sheepskin cloak** and **women's wool stockings.**

Men wearing women's stockings is part of a tradition of **male and female dual identity** at carnival time.

On Monday night, a **man made of straw** is carried on a cart to the centre of Mohács, where it is burned on top of a **bonfire** while people dance round it.

There's **lots of drinking** during the week of Busójárás, especially by the Busós. Visitors might find it difficult not to become involved in the festivities, since drunken Busós often drag unwitting tourists into the parades.

133

World
Testicle
Cooking
Championships

Villages of Ozrem and Lunjevica, Serbia
September

Ljubomir Erovic created a testicle-cooking festival in 2004. The full name is The World Championship of Cooking Aphrodisiacs and Testicle Specialties, which is more to the point: promoting natural food as a way to better sex. (Among other names, it's also referred to as the Balls Cup.) Most of the competing cooks are men, and most of the people attending are women.

134

It's a three-day festival:

FRIDAY
Competitors set up **Balls Cup Camp,** also known as the Balling Village; basically it's a tent city. A separate camp is set up by and for visitors who are not cooking. Get there early for the best places.

SATURDAY
This is the **actual competition:** cooking, judging, and the announcement of winners, followed by a rock concert in the evening.

SUNDAY
Everyone feasts on testicle pizzas, testicle goulash, or whatever dish is prepared by the winning team.

THE RULES
- **Only balls from animals that we already eat are allowed.** These are the animals whose balls have been cooked since the competition started.

- Participants must register their teams 10 days before the festival.

- Only one testicle recipe per competitor can be entered for judging.

- Ball meals must be cooked over **open fires;** no electricity or gas.

- Participants wishing to **test aphrodisiac effects** must retire to the Balling Village.

- Anyone over 65 is prohibited, unless they have doctor's permission.

- Viagra is prohibited.

Bull

Shark

Ram

Rooster*

Donkey

Ostrich*

Bear

Reindeer

Roe deer

Stallion

Turkey*

Elk

Goat

Pig

Wild boar

Swan*

Kangaroo

Rabbit

Mouflon

Badger

*Yes, they have balls; inside, near their kidneys.

The winner of **best testicle concoction** is awarded the official Ball Cup trophy:

In polite society, animals' balls are called **white kidneys,** so if you see that on a menu, you know what you are really getting.

Before cooking balls, you must **peel off the outer skin,** then soak them for 24 hours in a mixture of water (⅔) and wine (⅓), with garlic, pepper, and your choice of spices. (You can substitute lemon juice for the wine.)

Ask your local butcher for testicles (sometimes you'll get them free). But don't forget that **as well as testosterone, balls are very rich in cholesterol.**

At the festival you'll find a variety of dishes, including **testicles in béchamel sauce,** flavored with local herbs.

135

Air Guitar
World Championships

Norway

Russia

Sweden

Finland

Oulu, Finland
August

The Air Guitar World Championships have been taking place in Oulu since 1996, as part of the Oulu Music Video Festival. According to the organizers, the ideology behind the event was that "wars would end and all bad things would go away if everyone just played air guitar."

136

Gender equality
Men take the prize most years, but a female 19-year-old Japanese air guitarist was the 2014 World Champion. Between 5,000 and 6,000 people saw her winning performance.

The Rules

Instrument

- The instrument must be **invisible,** i.e. air.
- The contestant can use an electric or an acoustic air guitar, or both. Real picks may be used.
- Personal air roadies are allowed, but not back-up bands.

Finalists

- **National champions and the reigning world champion** are admitted directly into the Grand Final.
- Other contestants can qualify in the Dark Horses round, held the day before the Grand Final.

The program

- Contestants perform two 60-second songs in two separate rounds: one of these is the contestant's choice, and the other they only hear immediately before being asked to perform it.
- The five-person jury considers originality, mimesmanship, stage presence, technical merit, and airness, then gives contestants marks from 4.0 to 6.0 for each round.
- The winner gets an actual instrument (a custom-made Flying Finn guitar).

The countries taking part in air guitar championships vary from year to year, but have included Australia, Belgium, Brazil, Canada, France, Germany, Greece, Japan, Norway, Russia, Thailand, the Netherlands, the US, and, of course, Finland.

At the Helsinki Science Center there's a participatory exhibit that's pretty close to **a real air guitar.** An infrared camera recognizes the distance and movements between two special gloves worn by the participant and translates them into electric guitar sounds.

Wife Carrying World Championship

Norway

Russia

Sweden

Finland

Sonkajärvi, Finland
July

Locals started this event in 1992. In 1996, it became an international affair, and now attracts couples from Australia, Central Europe, North and South America, and countries all over the world. Legend has it that Ronkainen, a 19th-century villain, stole women from the area and carried them away.

*Many of the winners are from Estonia.

138

The organizers offer these tips on how to become a **Master in Wife Carrying:**

- The event is composed of humor and hard sport on a 50:50 basis. Everybody may choose what attitude to take towards the competition.

- Rhythm is very important. If the wife doesn't move with the carrier's rhythm, speed is slower. But when rhythm is mutual, carrier and wife become one, complementing the motions of the other.

The two-day festivities also include a **race for teams,** in which three men take turns in carrying the wife. Prior to each exchange, the next carrier has to drink the official "wife-carrying drink" before continuing.

Total length of the track (part sandy, part asphalt) is 0.25 mi (400 m).

The organizing committee has this **tip for wives:**

- Carrying birch switches is useful. (For whipping.)

Part of the course goes through 3 ft (1 m) of water. Wives with flexible backs have an advantage here!

As well as the wet part, the course includes two obstacles made from logs.

Carrying can be by any method.
Here are two of the most common:

Estonian Carry

Fireman's Lift

This one frees up the carrier's hands.

The couple with the fastest time wins.
The prize is the weight of the wife in beer.

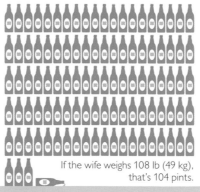

If the wife weighs 108 lb (49 kg), that's 104 pints.

(as set by The Official International Wife Carrying Competition Rules Committee)

- The wife to be carried may be your own, the neighbor's, or you may have found her farther away; she must, however, be over 17 years of age.

- The only equipment allowed is a belt worn by the carrier.

- All the participants must have fun.

- The contestants run the race two at a time, so each heat is a contest in itself.

- The minimum weight of the wife to be carried is 108 lb (49 kg). If she weighs less, she will be burdened with a heavy rucksack to reach the desired minimum weight.

139

Mobile Phone Throwing
World Championships

Norway

Russia

Sweden

Finland

Savonlinna, Finland
Late August

The interest
in throwing
phones erupted in
2000 when
Fennolingua,
a Finnish translation
company, organized
the first world
championships. Now
there are national
championships
all over Europe;
victors in those
contests win trips
to Savonlinna.

Original phones, with
batteries, are provided;
they weigh 0.5 lb (0.2 kg) or more,
and competitors can pick
any one they like the look of.

There are **four categories**
of competition:

JUNIORS
- 12 years and under
- one throw per competitor
- traditional over-the-
  shoulder throw
- longest throw wins

FREESTYLE
- no age limit
- individual and team events
- one throw per competitor
- style and aesthetics are judged
- graded from 1 to 6 points
- highest score wins

ORIGINAL
(men and women separate)
- one throw per competitor
- traditional over-the-
  shoulder throw
- longest throw wins

TEAM ORIGINAL
(max three to a team; can include
men and women)
- one throw per competitor
- traditional over-the-
  shoulder throw
- longest total of team's
  throws wins

What happens to all the phones?

The event was originally started by Nokia as a way to **recycle** phones. Apparently, instead of being recycled, phones were being thrown into lakes all over Finland, where their **batteries** become **toxic waste.**

In landfills, a large percentage of the toxic waste is electronic components (not all from phones, of course). The Mobile Phone-Throwing World Championships are **doing their bit to stop** toxic elements (and fumes when the stuff is burned) from **polluting our air and water.**

Other countries

with phone-throwing events include:

- Belgium
- Canada
- Czech Republic
- India
- Liechtenstein
- Norway
- Spain
- UK
- US

World records
(as of 2017)

Men: 362.3 ft (110.4 m)
(That's longer than a soccer field.)
Women: 222.6 ft (67.58 m)

141

Rouketopolemos
Rocket war

Vrontados, Greece
Easter

In the 19th century, the Ottoman occupiers of Chios imposed restrictions on the island's Easter church services.

This resulted in a "rocket war" between the villagers of Vrontados.

The Agios Marcos church is about 0.25 mi (400 m)…

At the same time as banning Easter services, **Ottoman occupiers confiscated all the weapons in Vrontados,** in case the villagers started an uprising against the ban.

In response, to scare the Turks, villagers started a **fake civil war** of sorts, firing homemade rockets much like the ones used in modern firework displays.

It worked! The local residents were once again able to celebrate Good Friday and Easter Sunday at their respective churches.

The two churches and nearby buildings are protected by metal sheets.

from the Erithiani church. Both were built on hilltops.

Nowadays, teams from the Eastern Orthodox churches of **Agios Marcos** (St. Mark) and **Erithiani** (the Virgin Mary) start preparing their rockets for the following year as soon as the current year's "war" is over.

Gunpowder is tamped down into cardboard tubes, which are fixed to long wooden sticks.

Between 8 pm on Holy Saturday and 12.30 am on Easter Sunday, the **two teams fire roughly 60,000 rockets at each other's churches.** The team that hits the other church's bell tower first is the winner.

Since both teams always claim to be the winner, they agree to settle their argument following year. And so the tradition continues.

Yağlı Güreş
Oil wrestling
Kırkpınar games

Turkey

**Edirne,
Turkey**
Early summer

Oil wrestling is the Turkish national sport. The Kırkpınar tournament has been held every year since 1362, making it the oldest sporting event in the world that's still going strong.

The three-day elimination tournament takes place in a large grassy arena.

Before the fight, **wrestlers pour olive oil over each other.**

They wear leather pants called *kisbet,* stretching from just below the navel to just below the knee. Traditionally they are made from water buffalo hides.

Wrestlers are allowed to put their arms inside the *kisbet* for a better grip. (However, grabbing an opponent's balls is thankfully prohibited.)

Each pair has an **assigned referee.** The wrestlers are not confined to a particular place in the arena, so the referee must follow them around, sometimes running after them to keep up.

A win is scored when…
- a wrestler turns his opponent's navel "to the heavens."
- an opponent gives up.
- a fighter is able to lift his opponent off the ground, and carry him five paces.
- a *kisbet* is dragged down so far that the fighter would expose himself when he stood up. (If you lose your trousers, you lose the bout.)

Originally, bouts had no time limit (they could go for a whole day), but in **1975 they were limited to 30 min** in the initial rounds, and 40 min in the finals.

If there's still no winner, the wrestlers re-oil each other and the bout continues. Then it's a **sudden death overtime:** the first wrestler to bring his opponent to the ground is the winner.

An important part of the whole event is the **respect and compassion** that wrestlers show for each other. After each bout the winner hugs the loser, and they walk out of the arena arm in arm.

Oil wrestling festivals have historically been held in **Greece** and **Macedonia**; more recently, this slippery sport has become popular in the **Netherlands** and **Japan.**

Deve Güreşi
Camel wrestling

Turkey

Selçuk, Turkey
3rd Sunday in January
(There are also roughly
30 camel wrestling
competitions each
year from November
to March in
Aegean Turkey.)

Male camels fight
naturally in the wild
—over females,
what else? Formal
competitions were
organized by Turkic
tribes more than
2,400 years ago.
Camel fighting was
discouraged in the
1920s as too
backward, but the
sport was revived in
the 1980s as
part of Turkey's
historic culture.

A female camel in heat is paraded nearby and **two bull camels** fight it out. (Sometimes there's fighting between owners, too.)

During the fight, camels foam at the mouth, **spraying saliva** all over the place.

Also, camels are retromingent, which means they **urinate backwards**. Spectators are advised to remember this.

Spectators might also want to beware of camels fleeing the fighting area. (Perhaps there's a catchphrase here: **peeing and fleeing**.)

There are about 2,000 wrestling camels in Turkey. They are bred for competition, and wrestle in the same weight class. They start fighting around age 10, and continue for 10 years.

Some camels attack their opponents from the right, some from the left. Some try to trip their opponents; some just try to push them over.

A **winner is declared** when the competitor:

- falls to the ground
- flees from the fight
- screams!

And if a camel's owner feels that his animal is in danger, he can **throw a rope onto the fighting area,** giving the victory to his opponent.

Camel owners often **name their animals** after politicians and world leaders.

Before the fights, the animals are draped in decorative rugs and take part in **camel beauty pageants.**

Events always take place on **Sundays,** usually in football stadiums. Individual fights last for 10 min each. If no camels have fallen over, run away, or screamed in that time, they are judged on a points system, based on their moves and agility.

Camel meat is served to spectators at certain events.

Animal rights organizations consider the sport **cruel.**

Just a little reminder: **camels have one hump…**

dromedaries have two humps.

147

Africa, Asia and Oceania

Deegal*
Crossing of the cattle

AFRICA

Mali

Diafarabé, Mali
Late December
or early January
(The date, always a
Saturday, is set when the
water level in the River
Niger is just right.)

Since Diafarabé was
founded in 1818,
the Deegal has been
the most important
festival for Fulani
tribesmen and their
herds. During the
rainy season, the
River Niger floods
the area, driving the
cattle north, but
when the monsoon is
over the water level
drops. This allows
the herds to return
home across the river.

*Also called Dewgal.

150

BAMAKO
(Capital of Mali)

R. Niger

Ségou

Fulani herders cross the river
with their herds, beating the
water with sticks to keep the
cattle together as a group.

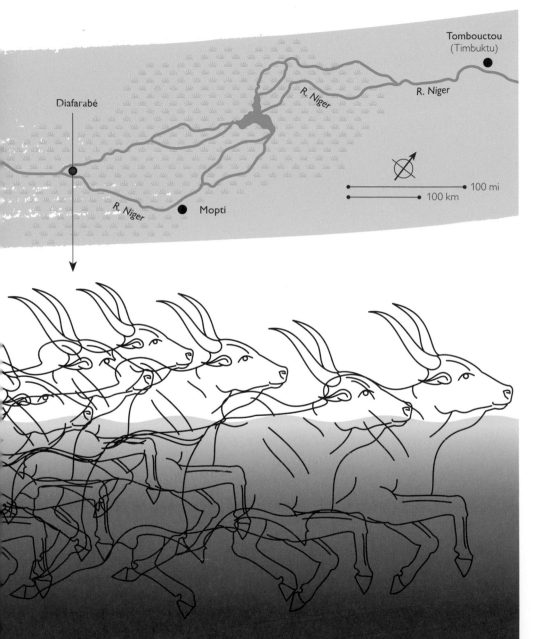

Tombouctou
(Timbuktu)

R. Niger

R. Niger

Diafarabé

R. Niger

Mopti

100 mi
100 km

Cattle cross the Niger in many places, but **Diafarabé is always the first** because the Niger inland delta begins there.

The goal is to get to the best grazing grounds (burgu).

There's a strict order of crossing:

- cattle that belong to village chiefs

- cattle that belong to powerful Muslim holy men

- cattle that belong to the head herder in charge of the *burgu* pastures

- cattle that belong to everyone else.

The Competition
When the crossing is complete, a panel of judges decides which animals are in the best condition and their herder is named **Best Caretaker.**

151

Cure Salée
Festival of the Nomads

AFRICA

Ingal, Niger
September

Started hundreds of years ago, this annual three-day gathering of the Tuareg and Wodaabe tribes takes place when the rainy season ends. It includes a beauty pageant for men, known as the Guéréwol, reflecting the cultural importance of beauty in the traditions of the region.

The Tuareg, and much smaller Wodaabe tribes, meet at the Ingal salt flats (*cure salée* means salt cure in French) to **prepare their herds of cattle and goats for the trip south,** where they'll live through the coming dry season.

The government of Niger has tried to promote the festival as a tourist attraction for Western visitors. This is not particularly welcomed by the tribespeople.

Various organizations, including UNICEF, use the Cure Salée to promote and **provide aid to curb HIV, malaria, Guinea worm, and malnutrition.**

The Cure Salée is also a **social gathering:** after living apart for months, the tribes share news and trade amongst themselves. The tiny town of Ingal (population: 500) grows to 50,000.

For the Wodaabe people it's a time of **courtship and marriage.**

During the **Guéréwol** beauty pageant, men paint their faces with **elaborate red and black makeup,** wear **traditional headdresses,** and take part in dancing and tests of skill (known as Yaake) to attract the attention of Wodaabe women seeking husbands. Some of the women are already married; **taking a second or third husband is OK in Wodaabe culture,** as long as the new one is good-looking.

Symmetry of facial features is highly valued by Wodaabe women, and the men's makeup empasizes this.

Part of Guéréwol involves many hours of dancing. To help their efforts, the men **drink a tea made from fermented bark.** It's thought to have hallucinogenic powers.

152

Although it is officially limited to three days, the Cure Salée can **last for weeks** while the nomadic groups stay in Ingal.

153

Evala
Wrestling
initiation rite

AFRICA

Togo

Kara, Togo
July

The two weeks
of Evala come
at the end of a long
initiation rite for
young Kabyè men.
In the week before
the event they isolate
themselves, eat lots
of dogmeat* and
refrain from sex, they
don't even shake
hands with girls,
before wrestling each
other for the right to
choose a wife.

*See the column
over there. ---------->

154

Eating dogs?

While dogmeat is a common food in this part of the world, it's a controversial part of this event and is not always acknowledged by Evala officials for fear it would offend the many tourists who come to watch.

The young wrestlers believe that eating dogmeat gives them **endurance** for the fights, and also that it imbues them with doggy attributes: **loyalty, courage, intelligence, cunning,** and **faithfulness.**

Before each fight, wrestlers are **smeared with fat** from a dead dog, making it hard to get a good grip on each others' slippery bodies.

155

Dinka and Bodi Fat Man Contests

Villages in South Sudan (the Dinka tribe) and Ethiopia (Bodi)
Part of the New Year ceremony in June

The opposite of dieting, their goal is to honor those who get really fat.

There's one difference between the two competitions: in South Sudan, the **Dinka tribesmen have four months** to get as fat as they can; in Ethiopia, the **Bodi men take six months.**

Each village chooses an unmarried competitor, who must retire to his hut, lie down, eat and drink pretty much continuously, and stay completely immobile, for instance, no sex is allowed, so they **burn as few calories as possible.**

Women bring the food and drink to the men. In Ethiopia, what they drink is a mixture of **cow's blood and milk.** The first 4.2 pt (2 L) drink is at sunrise, and because it's hot in that part of the world, it must be downed quickly before it coagulates. (In South Sudan, it's just cow's milk.)

Because cows are sacred, the blood is taken from a vein, which is stopped up with clay afterwards.

Some men almost double their weight. One year, a competitor's belly ruptured just before the judging. The dead man was awarded the fattest man honor.

A F R I C A

On the day of the ceremony, the men cover themselves in ashes and white clay and stagger out of their huts, usually with a stick to steady them since the muscles in their legs have withered from lack of exercise. They then **parade naked round a sacred tree** for their girth and size to be judged by the community.

The winner gets no prize, but is fêted for the rest of his life. Also, fat people are considered to be rich. **Young women hope to marry a fat man** (after he's lost the weight).

And, in fact, **most men do lose the weight** they have gained in about the same time they took to put it on. Of course, if they don't win the competition they'll probably try to be their village's entrant next year.

The Dinka are among the **tallest people on Earth.** Manute Bol, one of the two tallest-ever basketball players in the US—at 7 ft 7 in (2.4 m)—was a Dinka.

Here's how he (dotted line) compares to a competitive fat man.

The government of South Sudan has tried to ban the fattening contests on the grounds that they promote laziness. During the 2016 contest, though, 17 Dinka men were arrested for trying to make themselves fat.

The photographer Eric Lafforgue has chronicled the Fat Man Contest. This black silhouette is based on one of his pictures.

Mwaka Kogwa
Show of the year

Makunduchi,
Zanzibar Island, Tanzania
July

In this event, which has origins in the Persian New Year celebrations of the Shirazi people, men swat each other with banana stalks. Later, they set fire to a small thatched hut. It happens all over Tanzania, but the best place to watch the event is in Makunduchi, in the south of the Tanzanian island of Zanzibar, just off the east coast of Africa.

Banana stalks are the parts of the tree that bananas grow on (sort of upside down).

This part can also be used for making paper.

1

The fight between the men is a ritual designed to let everyone **air their grievances, and clear the air for the New Year.**

While the men fight, the women sing about life and love, dressed in their best and brightest clothes.

Predictions for the New Year are made according to the direction of the smoke.

Everyone is welcome at the festival. It's a local belief that anyone without a guest at Mwaka Kogwa is unhappy.

Tourists do not have to swat each other with banana stalks (or anything else).

2

After the fight, a **small thatched hut is built, set on fire, and then extinguished.** This ritual is said to ensure that no one will die if their house catches fire in the coming year.

Then the party moves to the beach, where there's a banquet and dancing.

Bokdrol Spoeg
Kudu
dung spitting

Kirkwood, South Africa
Throughout the year (Best times for hunting kudu are May through November.)

In 1994, the Afrikaner community in South Africa made a formal sport out of something pretty disgusting that hunters had been doing for ages: they put kudu dung pellets into their mouths and spit them out as far as they can.

The rules are simple:

- Put dung pellet in mouth.
- Spit it out.
- The longest spit wins.

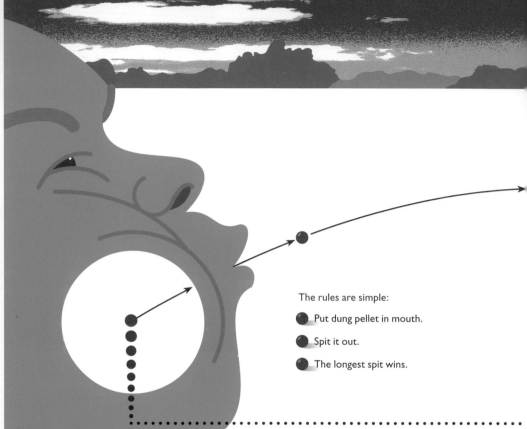

To make the process slightly more palatable:
National Geographic has reported that dropping the pellet into a shot of alcohol then catching it in the teeth while swallowing the liquid minimizes the taste and helps sterilize the dung.

Oh, those humans; what silly games they play.

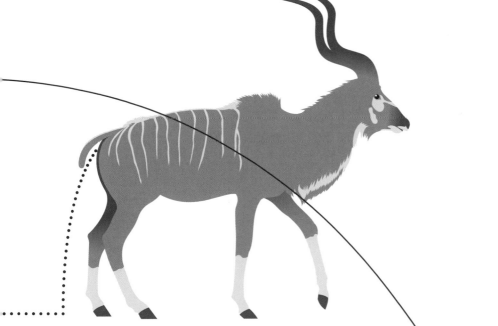

Kudu, a type of antelope, are difficult animals to hunt, but they leave a trail of dung pellets as they try to escape hunters. The hunters invented the game as a way to pass the time while trying to find the kudu.

Piece of shit, actual size

In 2015, a **sheep** dung spitting contest was held at the Lady of the Lake Festival in Irvinestown, **Northern Ireland.**

During the competition, the organizer was photographed on the ground at the south end of a sheep with dung pellets on his face. Really.

Distance records for spitting other stuff:

Cherry stones 96 ft (29 m)
Watermelon seeds 69 ft (21 m)
Brown crickets 32 ft (9.8 m)
Tobacco juice 25 ft (7.5 m)

…and the world record for **kudu poop** is 51 ft (15.6 m).

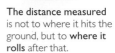

The distance measured is not to where it hits the ground, but to **where it rolls** after that.

Basant*
Panchami
Kite Flying
Festival

**Amritsar, India
(And throughout India
and parts of Pakistan)**
Spring
(*Basant* means spring,
Panchami is the 5th day
of *Maagh*, the Sikh
month that corresponds
to late January or
early February.)

**Started as a fair in
the 19th century,
Basant Panchami is
a secular holiday in
many parts of India.
In the Punjab region
of India (and the
Punjab province
in Pakistan) the
holiday is famous
for kite flying.**

*Also Vasant

162

Lahore, Pakistan, used to be one of the most spectacular kite-flying venues. But all kites were banned there in 2007, following several deaths caused by cuts from special kite strings *(dorr)* that were threaded with pieces of glass. These dangerous *dorr* were used to cut the strings of other people's kites, in what was once seen as a friendly competition.

The tradition of cutting kite strings continues in Amritsar. Strings also break when they become entangled. If this happens, the winner shouts *"Bo Kata,"* while the loser reels in the string as fast as possible, then fetches the kite and starts again.

Most of the kite flyers are young women, who wear **yellow** to honor the birthday of the goddess **Saraswati,** and to celebrate the annual **mustard crop,** welcoming spring.

Mallakhamb
Pole gymnastics
Delhi, India
National championships and various events during the year throughout India

Mallakhamb was first mentioned in the 12th century; it was revived as an art form in the 19th century, and in 1958, a competitive version was introduced at the National Gymnastics Championships in Delhi.

There are three disciplines, using different **equipment:**

- **Plain Mallakhamb**
  A teak pole is fixed to the ground.
- **Hanging Mallakhamb**
  A pole shorter than the fixed one hangs down leaving a space of about 3 ft (1 m) between it and the ground. The swinging motion of this Mallakhamb makes exercises harder than on the fixed pole.
- **Rope Mallakhamb**
  A cotton rope replaces the pole. Performers must execute poses without knotting the rope.

In competition, 90-second routines are judged on:

- **speed**
- **grace**
- **difficulty**

8.5 ft
(2.5 m)

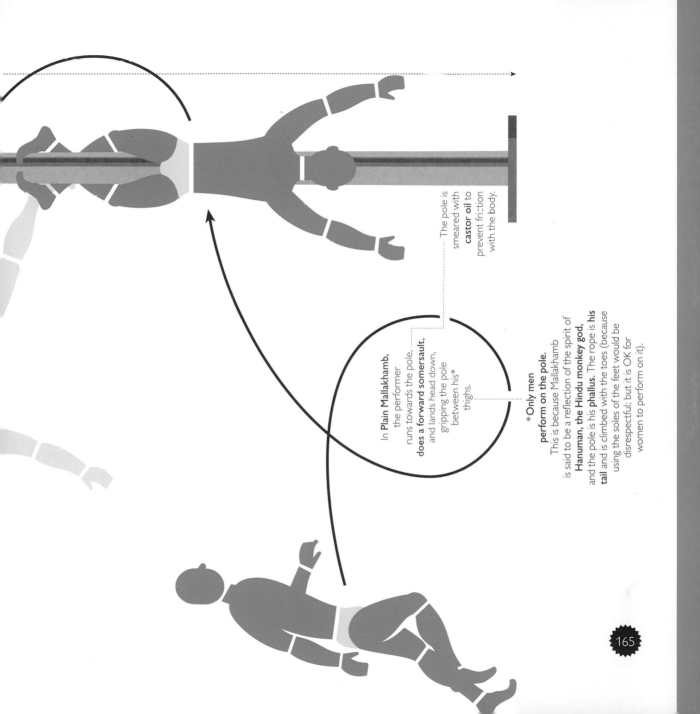

The pole is smeared with **castor oil** to prevent friction with the body.

In **Plain Mallakhamb,** the performer runs towards the pole, **does a forward somersault,** and lands head down, gripping the pole between his* thighs.

*Only men perform on the pole.
This is because Mallakhamb is said to be a reflection of the spirit of **Hanuman, the Hindu monkey god,** and the pole is his **phallus.** The rope is his **tail** and is climbed with the toes (because using the soles of the feet would be disrespectful; but it is OK for women to perform on it).

Dahi Handi*
Human pyramids

India

**Mumbai,
India**
Late August

Legend says that as a child Krishna loved butter and curd so much he stole it from the earthenware pots that were used to process and store milk products. In an effort to stop this, cowherds hung the pots up high, but Krishna and his buddies formed human pyramids and climbed up to reach them.

This is what's reenacted during Dahi Handi.

*Dahi = curd
Handi = earthen pot

166

Dahi Handi is part of the Gokulashtami festival, a celebration of Krishna's birth. Young men form themselves into human towers of up to **nine tiers**—roughly 43 ft (13 m) high.

Team members are called Govinda Pathaks (Govinda is a name for Krishna). They practice building their pyramids for months. During the festivities, they get **three tries** to reach a *handi*.

Historically, a small child climbed up the human pyramid to reach the earthen pot *(handi)*, but the Supreme Court of India recently ruled that **children must be over 12** to take part.

It's a crush: imagine yourself here!

When the *handi* is smashed open, **buttermilk** gushes out and flows down the pyramid, symbolizing the team's collaborative effort.

Earthenware *handis* are set up all over Mumbai, and teams of youths travel round the city trying to break as many of them as they can.

Women (representing the original cowherds who were annoyed because their curds were being stolen by Krishna) **throw water** on the pyramid as it is being formed, making it slippery and difficult for team members to hold onto each other.

This has led to **many injuries** over the years. Some groups advocate lowering the height at which the *handis* are hung.

Apart from curds, there's **money to be won,** and this makes the competition all the more intense.

Political parties and celebrities endorse the main event in Mumbai, where hundreds of teams (called *mandals*) compete for prize money that has reached 10 million rupees.

Ritual Baby Dropping

Sri Santeswar Temple,
Karnataka State, India
December

Believed to bring health and good luck to babies, this tradition has existed for about 100 years (and some say it's much older).

A similar ceremony took place in Solapur, Maharashtra State, at the shrine of Baba Umer Dargah. The practice was banned there in 2011, but continues today in small villages within Karnataka and Maharashtra States.

Although both Muslim and Hindu communities take part, the ritual isn't part of either religion's classical traditions.

The drop is about 30 ft (9 m).

2

A priest performs the next part. First he grips the baby by the ankles and wrists. Then, holding him or her horizontally and facing up, the **priest swings the baby back and forth** while chanting prayers. Finally, he **lets the baby fall.**

1

A religious **devotee** climbs the temple wall (on a rope or ladder) **with a bucket slung across his back. The baby is inside the bucket.**

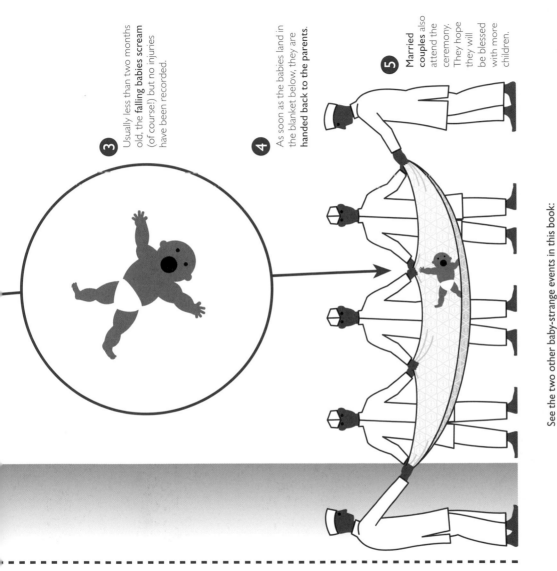

3

Usually less than two months old, the **falling babies scream** (of course!) but no injuries have been recorded.

4

As soon as the babies land in the blanket below, they are **handed back to the parents**.

5

Married couples also attend the ceremony. They hope they will be blessed with more children.

See the two other baby-strange events in this book:

El Colacho in Spain (p. 102), in which a man jumps over babies lying in the street, and the **Nakizumo Festival** in Japan (p. 194), in which sumo wrestlers try to make babies cry just by looking at them.

Holi
The Hindu
Festival of Colors
(or Festival of Love)

India

**All over
the country**
The start of spring

The last full moon of
the month, Falgun in
the Hindu lunar
calendar (usually in
March), marks the
beginning of spring.

Bonfires are lit the
night before to
celebrate the triumph
of Prahlada (good)
over Holika (the
demoness). The next
day the fun begins:
everyone throws
colored powder and
water at each other.

170

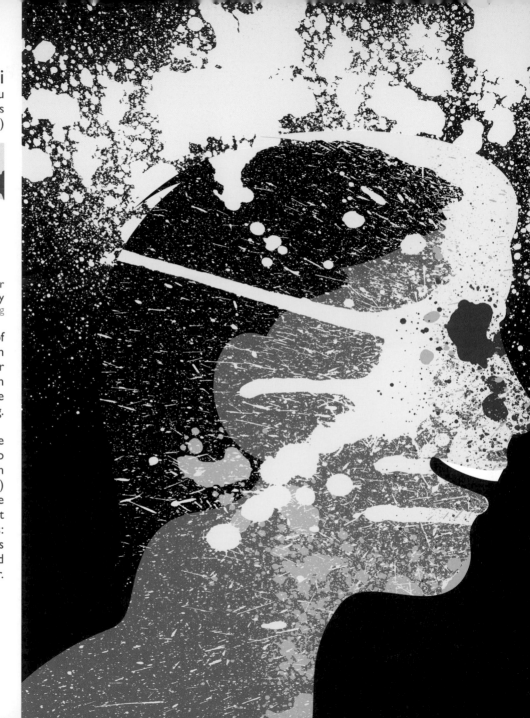

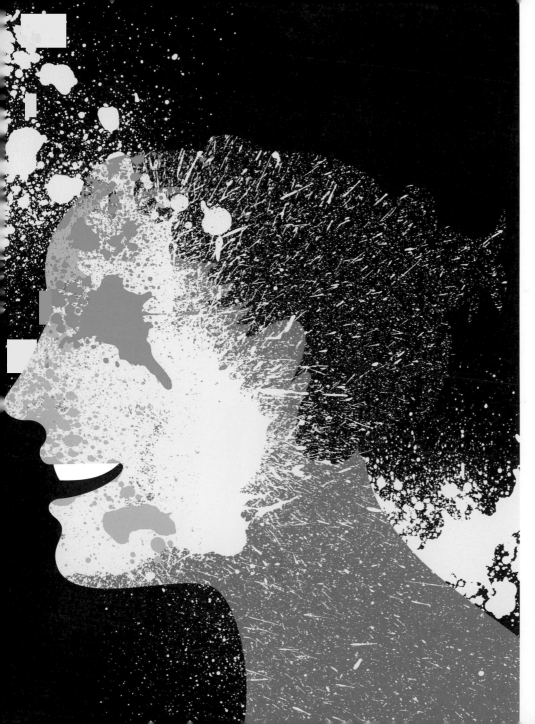

There's lots of **singing and dancing** too.

Revellers drink *bhang,* made from cannabis leaves. It's mixed into sweet drinks and takes the edge off the mess you are in.

Until recently widows were excluded from the festivities but now they throw color with abandon.

Holi is also popular among non-Hindus, in countries including **South Africa** and the **US.**

Laundry bills are huge.

171

Kandy Esala Perahera*
Elephant parade

India

Kandy,
Sri Lanka
July or August
(depending on
the full moon)

Five elephant
processions, with
fire dancers, whip
crackers, drummers,
acrobats and sword
twirlers between
the separate groups,
pay homage to the
Sacred Tooth
of Lord Buddha.
The whole
thing lasts for
10 consecutive
nights.

*Esala = month
of celebrations and
festivities in the
Sinhalese calendar
Perahera = parade

About **50 well-dressed elephants** take part. Many of them have electric lights embedded in their face masks.

Drummers and other performers in the processions **clear the way** for the elephants.

The legend of the Sacred Tooth

When **Buddha** was cremated in the 5th century BCE, someone took a tooth from the funeral pyre. It was later **smuggled into Sri Lanka,** hidden in the hair of a princess who was disguised as a priest.

The King of Sri Lanka was pleased to have the relic in his kingdom, so he paraded it through the streets of Kandy for all to see. Today a replica tooth goes on parade (inside a golden casket), while the original remains in the **Temple of the Tooth Relic** (Sri Dalada Maligwawa).

Cutting the water

On the morning after the tenth day of processions there's a ceremony in which a religious official **draws a sword through the Mahaweli Ganga (river),** to divide pure from impure, and ensure a continuing supply of water for the coming year.

173

Naadam
Three games of men

Russia

Mongolia

China

Ulaanbaatar, Mongolia
July 11–13

Genghis Kahn presided over the first official Naadam in the 13th century. For centuries before that, the games had celebrated weddings and clan gatherings. In addition to the sports, it was a way for Kahn to enlist soldiers for his army. The modern event started in 1921, recognizing the country's indepen-dence from China.

The three games are an Eastern version of the ancient Olympics. **They were originally just for men,** but women now take part in archery and **horse racing.** Celebrations and sports events are held in many parts of the country, but the largest, the **National Naadam,** is held in the National Sports Stadium in Ulaanbaatar, the country's capital. After an **opening ceremony** with dancers, musicians, athletes, and riders, the games begin.

In 2010, Naadam became part of UNESCO's Representative List of Intangible Cultural Heritage of Humanity.

1 MONGOLIAN TRADITIONAL WRESTLING matches have **no time limit, and no size classification:** the wrestler with the greatest fame has the privilege of picking his opponent. There are 9 or 10 rounds (depending on the total number of wrestlers).

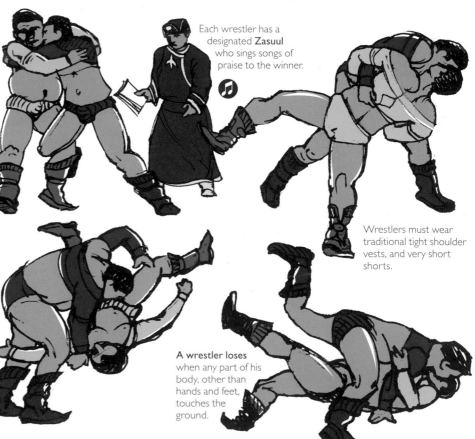

Each wrestler has a designated **Zasuul** who sings songs of praise to the winner.

Wrestlers must wear traditional tight shoulder vests, and very short shorts.

A wrestler loses when any part of his body, other than hands and feet, touches the ground.

Prizes for winners include wonderful titles, such as:

- Eye-Pleasing Nationally Famous Mighty Invincible Giant

② MONGOLIAN HORSE RACING is a long-distance, cross-country event, with races 9–18 mi (15–30 km) long. About 1,000 horses from anywhere in Mongolia participate in the Naadam.

Mongolian horses are small and are **ridden by children aged 5 to 13 years old.** They train for months before the races, which are determined by their horse's age. (Younger horses run shorter races.)

 For good luck, jockeys sing the song "Ginko" to their horses before they race.

③ ARCHERY competitors are members of 10-person teams. They each get **four arrows,** made from willow branches and vulture feathers, to shoot at the targets.

Archers sing to their arrows for a straight flight, while judges sing praise for successful shots. There's clearly a lot of singing at Naadam.

A leather shield is worn to keep the loose, traditional clothing out of the way.

5 ft (1.5 m)

The **targets** are small woven or wooden cylinders (*surs*), placed one on top of another to make a low wall. The idea is to hit *surs* out of the wall.

Men shoot their arrows from 246 ft (75 m) away; **women** shoot from 213 ft (65 m).

175

Da Shuhua
Festival of lights

Nuanquan, China
15th day of Chinese
New Year celebrations
in February

This 300-year-old
tradition dates from
a time when the
villagers of Nuanquan
couldn't afford
fireworks for New
Year's festivities. As
a substitute, they
collected scrap metal
and gave it to local
blacksmiths, who
melted it down and
threw it onto the
village's brick gate.
Today, it's more
popular than the
firework displays
in the village.

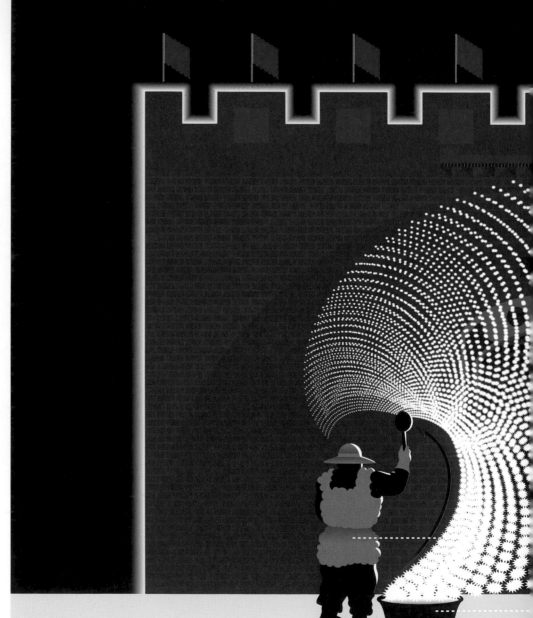

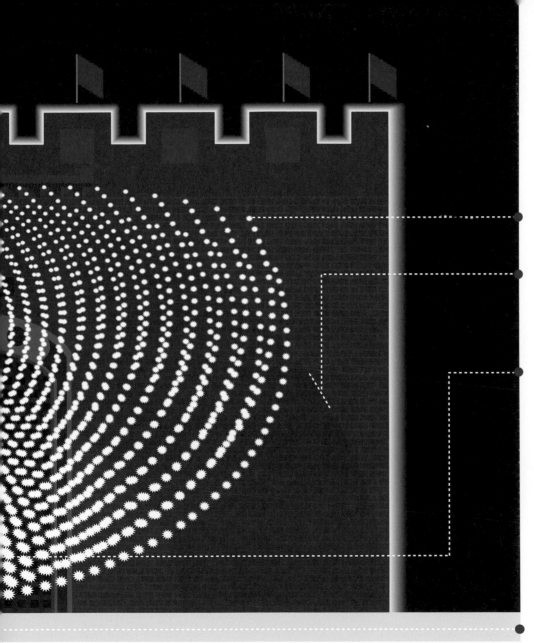

Before the big event, **musicians and dancers perform** in front of the village gate. Then…

cauldrons of molten metal are carried out, and the blacksmiths start to throw it at the wall in **huge sweeping arcs.** Sparks fly!

Over the years, a thin **skin of iron** has formed on the bricks.

The blacksmiths don't wear modern fireproof clothing—just simple, rough **sheepskin jackets and straw hats.** That may not seem like enough protection, but the men are skilled at handling the metal, and no one has ever been burned during the event.

Traditional wooden ladles that have been soaked for three days are used to throw the molten metal. A layer of coal forms on the ladles as soon as they contact it, stopping them from catching fire.

The metal is 1,832° F (1,000° C).

Bee Bearding

**Shaoyang City,
China**
July

Bee bearding
was introduced
in the **1830s** by
a Ukrainian bee-
keeper. It soon
became popular
in American
carnivals and
freak shows.

Today in
competition
(or in attempts to
claim a place in the
record books)
bees cover the
whole body, but
it's still called
"bearding."

The competition
winner is the one
who "wears"
the most bees,
by weight.

It takes roughly
350,000 bees to
cover the body.
Records are
much higher.

10,000 bees
weigh about
2.2 lbs (1 kg).

The *Guinness Book of Records* now has a competitor.
Carrying the Flag World Records, from China, details an even stranger
collection of human actions than its much older predecessor.

(The guy being stung below is Chinese,
and his record was reported
in the new book.)

How to take part
Potential bee-bearders,
read this first.

But...

do you
really want
to do this?

Before
- No showering;
  bees get excited
  by the smell of soap.
- Hang a small box
  around your neck with
  a queen bee inside it
  to attract other bees.*

During
- Stand still.
- Pray.
A new world record
of 240 lbs (109 kg) was
set in 2015 (equivalent
to 1.1 million bees).

After
- Accept medical help.
  The world record holder
  was stung 2,000 times.
  (But look on the bright
  side—that means
  1,098,000 bees did not
  sting him.)

Goggles,
ear- and
nose-plugs
are advised.

Smoking is optional,
but it did help
to stop this man
swallowing bees.

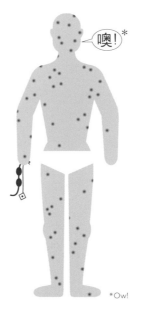

噢！*

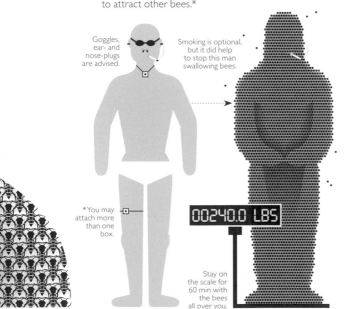

*You may
attach more
than one
box.

00240.0 LBS

Stay on
the scale for
60 min with
the bees
all over you.

*Ow!

A different beard

**The Clovermead Bee
Beard Competition
takes place annually
in Ontario, Canada.**

- Competitors
  come from all
  over the world,
  including Australia,
  England, and Israel.

- A team consists of
  a beekeeper (the
  bearder), and a bee
  whisperer who
  styles the beard.

- The teams go
  into a sealed tent
  to attract bees
  from their own
  hive and fashion
  the beard.

- 20 min later,
  the teams gather
  on a stage, and
  the bee-wearers
  perform a little
  dance in front of
  the spectators.

- Two judges
  award the
  championship to
  the wearer who
  does the best
  dance.

- Spectators pick a
  crowd favourite.

Songkran
Water festival

Myanmar
Laos
Vietnam
Thailand
Cambodia

Chiang Mai,*
Thailand
April 13–15
(Thai New Year)

Songkran was originally an occasion when Thai people poured water on statues of Buddha to represent purification and the washing away of sins and bad luck. Younger people traditionally poured water on the palms of older members of their families, as a way of showing respect.

*This is the biggest water festival in Thailand, but Bangkok and other cities also hold water events to mark the New Year.

The word **Songkran** comes from Sanskrit and is translated as "astrological passage" (the passage from Aries to Taurus). For Thai people it's a time for physical and spiritual spring cleaning.

Statues of Buddha are moved from local temples and paraded through the streets on April 13. Water is poured over the Buddhas' arms and legs as a sign of respect. But Songkran **continues for two more days,** and its religious origins are soon forgotten when the event turns into **a free-for-all water battle** with anyone you meet in the streets.

180

Clouds of white powder (talc or chalk) are thrown, as well as water. The streets look as though there's been a snowstorm.

If you go, wear **goggles,** because some of the water squirted at you may not be completely clean.

It's best to wear as little clothing as possible, but total **nudity is forbidden.**

The festival takes place at the **hottest time of the year,** so you may actually welcome getting soaked. **Be prepared:** veteran attendees with supersoakers like **this one** carry large supplies of water, and they won't hesitate to aim for you.

Apart from these relatively simple toys, the wet stuff is dispensed from every available container; people stand by the sides of the streets with **buckets and hoses** to drench passersby, and **trucks** with huge water tanks spray the crowds.

181

Monkey Banquet

Thailand

**Lopburi,
Thailand**
Last Sunday
in November

Started in **1989**,
this annual dinner
party honors
macaques and their
fellow primates,
which are ever-
present members
of Lopburi society.
And yes, it causes a
bit of a nuisance.

They might be pickpockets, but these **long-tailed macaques** are venerated by the local population of Lopburi, about 95 mi (150 km) north of Bangkok.

The macaques are thought to be descended from the **monkey god Hanuman,** and locals believe they bring fortune and good luck.

Among the believers is Yonyuth Kitwatananusont, owner of the Lopburi Inn. The monkeys had become a big tourist attraction for the city, making his business very successful, so he decided to throw a thank-you party for them.

The event starts at 10 am in the grounds of the **Phra Prang Sam Yot temple.**

First, there's music and dancing by humans dressed as monkeys, then at the dinner hour 3,000 real macaques appear and, though initially a bit timid, they soon dive into the buffet.

**How to behave
if you go to watch:**

- Don't look monkeys straight in the eye— they consider that a threat, and may attack.

- Don't bring any food in your back-pack or pockets. They *will* find it.

- Stay relaxed. Don't taunt.

- When the monkeys have become accustomed to the spectators, it's OK to feed them. Just be careful.

- You'll get a stick for self-defense with your entrance fee, but try not to use it. The ticket costs about 20 baht.

The spread of food includes sugary sodas and sweet desserts as well as fruit, so it's not surprising that pretty soon the macaques get an energy surge, and the whole thing turns into a **massive food fight.**

183

Pacu Jawi*
Cow racing

Malaysia

INDONESIA

Sumatra

**Tanah Datar,
West Sumatra,
Indonesia**
Held during 11
months of the year

Pacu Jawi is a
400-year-old
tradition in which
the Indonesian
Minangkabau people
celebrate the end of
the rice harvest.

Because Pacu Jawi
races are held in
11 different sub-
districts of Tanah
Datar, they take
place almost
monthly, in very
muddy rice paddies.

*Pacu = race
Jawi = cow or ox

It's all about the cows.
The idea is to get them to
run in a straight line across
a muddy field. One team
runs at a time, and the
fastest and strongest team
is crowned champion.

**Jockeys steer the teams
of two animals by holding
onto their tails.** At the
start of a run he bites the
tails for the same reason a
jockey riding a horse uses
a whip. (He might bite
the tails again during the
run to produce an extra
burst of speed.)

The **harness** is a
simplified version
of the one used
for ploughing.

The mud is
knee deep.
If a jockey
falls into it,
his race
is over.

184

Concentrating on the **straightness of the run,** and cooperation between the two cows (sometimes oxen are used) in the team, reflects the animals' everyday jobs: ploughing the rice paddies.

The muddy race fields vary in length from 66 ft (20 m) to 328 ft (100 m).

After a good run, the value of a cow increases greatly. A normal price is 7 million rupees, but it can rise to more than twice that for their breeder-owners.

It might appear the animals are having a rough time but this is misleading; they are clearly loved, as you can see when the jockeys carefully wash the mud off after the event to prepare them for inspection by potential buyers.

Panjat Pinang
Areca tree climbing competition

Villages in Indonesia
August 17
(Independence Day)

Climbing the greased, slippery trunk of an areca nut palm is a traditional event that celebrates Indonesia's independence.

It's a continuation of something the Dutch did to entertain themselves in the colonial era—watching local indigenous youths attempt to cling on to the tree (with many inevitably falling off)—and as such is slightly frowned upon these days as a degrading reminder of former Dutch rule.

Nevertheless, in order to reach the prizes hanging from the hoop at the top of the tree, a considerable amount of teamwork is needed. This is often cited as a good enough reason to continue the tradition. And it's all good, messy fun.

Areca trees are felled especially for the competitions. They are stripped, then covered with oil and other lubricants.

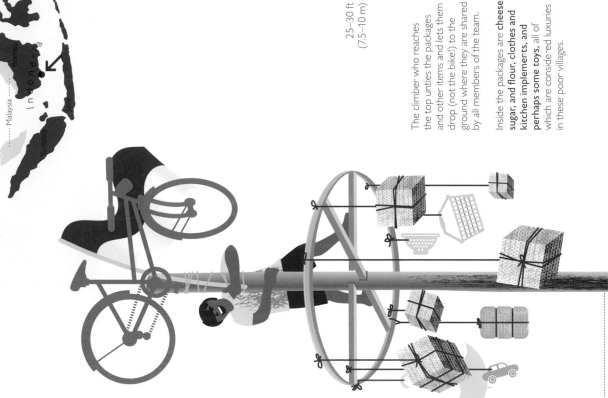

25–30 ft
(7.5–10 m)

The climber who reaches the top unties the packages and other items and lets them drop (not the bike!) to the ground where they are shared by all members of the team.

Inside the packages are cheese, sugar, and flour, clothes and kitchen implements, and perhaps some toys, all of which are considered luxuries in these poor villages.

Thailand

Malaysia

Indonesia

Borneo

Sumatra

Java

Heavier guys stand at the bottom of the pole, forming a solid base for the climbers.

In larger villages, several of the areca trees (or other substitute tree trunks) are erected, so many teams can compete for prizes.

More conservation-minded regions are starting to use **bamboo** trunks or **coconut** trees instead.

Nuts from the areca palm (usually called betel nuts) are wrapped in betel leaves and chewed like tobacco. The resulting juice, called *buai pekpek*, is bright red, and looks remarkably like blood when chewers spit it onto the ground.

Nuts

Many Indonesian regions disapprove of spitting.

But *buai pekpek* does have its uses: for tanning leather and as a dye.

187

Onzichtbare Sterren
Invisible stars

Borneo

Sulawesi

I n d o n e s i a

Java

**Fiapitú,
Indonesia**
April

After the eruption
of Mt. Semloh in
1815, stars were
blotted out at night
(and sun during the
day) for 48 hours
due to the mass
of ash thrown up
from the volcano.
The people of
nearby Fiapitú
remember the event
with the tradition
of Onzichtbare
Sterren.*

*They kept the old
Dutch name, a relic
of the time when
Indonesia was the
Dutch East Indies.

188

1 On the second
Tuesday in April,
**all street and house
lights are turned off**
in Fiapitú to simulate
the complete
blackout following
the 1815 eruption.

2 Men and women
wear **big stars.**

(Back view;
walking
takes some
practice.)

3 Families walk to neighbors'
houses, where they put **star
stickers on the doors.**

**Children under eleven
must wear blindfolds**
instead of stars, so they'll
learn what it's like when
the stars go out.

As is often the case, **commercialism** has somewhat overtaken the event, with local merchants selling star-themed *everything:* **sandwiches, haircuts, teeth implants, and tattoos,** as well as countless star-shaped trinkets.

In 1883, there was another major (though less deadly) volcanic eruption in **Krakatoa,** Indonesia, that caused a different kind of environmental change. **Skies around the world were tinted bright colors,** and it's thought that Edvard Munch reproduced these in the background of his famous 1893 painting *The Scream.*

4 Later, everyone goes to the town square to enact an *uitbarsting spel* (eruption play). One person is chosen to dress as Mt. Semloh. He (or she, in recent years) wears a breathing mask and operates a smoke machine inside the Semloh suit while the townspeople **throw star-shaped bread** into the opening.

5 **Bread represents the loss of crops** following the 1815 eruption. It caused widespread starvation in the region, but **sacrificing precious bread** is thought to ward off more deadly eruptions.

6 The following year, **1816, was known as the "year without a summer,"** because of the climate change that occurred around the world when immense amounts of ash were hurled into the upper atmosphere.

189

MassKara Festival
Smiling masks for everyone

Bacolod, Philippines
Closest weekend to October 19
(the city's Charter Day)

This festival was started by the city of Bacolod in 1980 to cheer its people up after two devastating events.

Civic figures and artists created this festival to overcome the economic hardship and loss of life, promoting Bacolod as **"the city of smiles,"** helping to put on a happy face in bad times.

Masskara is the Filipino word for mask, but it's also a play on the English word *mass* coupled with *kara* (*cara* means face in Spanish).

① **Sugar cane** used to be Bacolod's main agricultural crop, and the biggest employer. But the **price of sugar fell rapidly in the 1970s** due to increased worldwide use of substitutes like corn syrup. This led to economic downturn in the area.

② **In 1980,** the luxury liner *Don Juan* collided with a tanker and sank, resulting in **the death of hundreds of Negrenses** (people from the Negros province of the Philippines.)

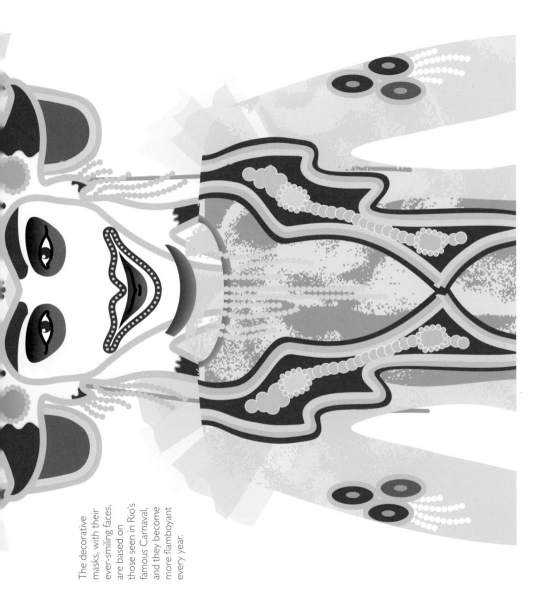

The decorative masks, with their ever-smiling faces, are based on those seen in Rio's famous Carnaval, and they become more flamboyant every year.

As well as the grand **parade of smiling masks,** the festival includes:

 street dance competitions in two categories—schools, and spectacular dances in the *barangays* (districts of the Philippines), which are the highlight of the competiton

the MassKara Queen beauty pageant

coconut milk drinking, pig catching, and **pole climbing** competitions

food festivals, **sports** events, **music** concerts, **agricultural** trade fairs

mask-making contests

Kanamara Matsuri
Festival of the phallus

Kawasaki, Japan
1st Sunday in April

The festival's origin dates from the 1600s as a celebration of sexual health and fertility.

An old story says that **the Kanayama Shinto shrine is dedicated to a blacksmith.** He had forged an iron dildo to break the teeth of a *vagina dentata* (toothed vagina), which had castrated two bridegrooms on their wedding nights.

The *vagina dentata* was a metaphor for syphilis, and it was protection from syphilis that prostitutes sought at the shrine, starting first during the Edo period (1603–1868).

Today, sex workers continue to visit the shrine to pray for protection.

The modern festival started in 1977. It gets going on Saturday evening, with everyone eating grilled rice treats in the shape of **yin and yang.** (Yin for female energy, yang for male.)

At 11 am on Sunday morning, there's a bonfire. **Sardines and sake are served.**

At noon, portable shrines (*mikoshi*) with giant phalluses are being paraded through town. This **pink penis** was donated by a drag queen club in Tokyo called Elizabeth Kaikan. Only drag queens are allowed to carry the special *mikoshi*.

Individual messages are attached to the statues, asking for **health, fertility and long, happy marriages.**

There's an **even bigger penis** at the Hōnen Matsuri (penis fertility festival) in Komaki, near Nagoya. That one is 15 ft (4.6 m) long. The one shown here is about 12 ft (3.6 m). I guess there will always be competition over-length.

192

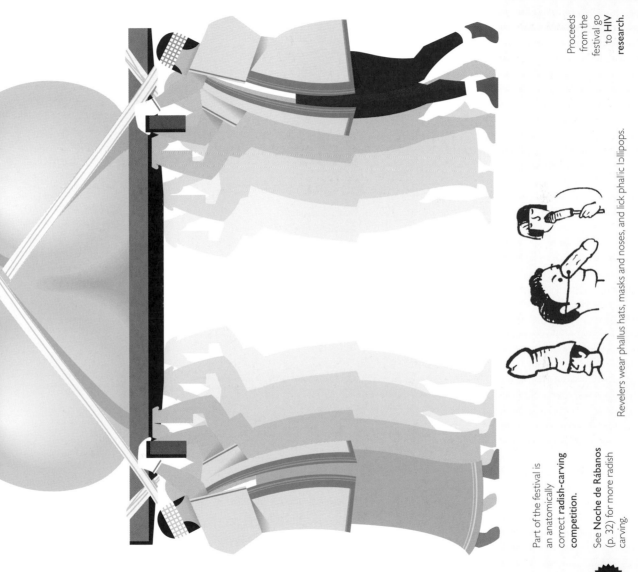

Part of the festival is an anatomically correct **radish-carving competition.**

See **Noche de Rábanos** (p. 32) for more radish carving.

Proceeds from the festival go to **HIV research.**

Revelers wear phallus hats, masks and noses, and lick phallic lollipops.

Nakizumo Festival
Making babies cry

Japan

Tokyo,
Japan
4th Sunday in April

A baby-crying competition is held on Japan's Children's Day holiday in the Buddhist Sonsoji Temple.

Two sumo wrestlers face each other holding babies and trying to make them cry by pulling faces and gentle jiggling.

Apparently **plenty of parents are willing to give up their babies** to the *sumotori* (student sumo wrestlers); in fact there's quite a contest to get a place. (Only 100 make it.)

All the children are under a year old.

The winning wrestler is the one whose baby cries first. (If both babies cry at the same time, the loudest is the winner.)

Nakizumo (literally: crying sumo) is a 400-year old tradition, but it's only been held in the modern age since 1991.

The idea that making babies cry is good, not awfully cruel, is based on the Japanese saying *naku ko wa sodatsu,* which means **crying babies grow fastest,** and the belief that their loud cries will scare away demons so they grow up healthy.

A **priest,** or *gyoji,* **acts as a referee,** shouting and sometimes waving at the babies to make their cries louder. If a student sumo wrestler fails to make his baby cry, the priest puts on a devil mask. That usually does the trick.

Naki!
Naki!
Naki!
(Cry! Cry! Cry!)

Onbashira
Honored pillars festival

Lake Suwa region of Nagano, Japan
Once every six years in April and May*

Dating back some **1,200 years,** Onbashira consists of two parts:

1. Yamadashi, in which huge trees are felled and hauled to Suwa.

2. Satobiki, where the logs are installed at four shrines.

*In Japan, they say Onbashira happens every seven years, because they count the current year in the total.

Suwa

Lake Suwa

NAGANO

Mt. Aka (Yatsugatake)

YAMANASHI

To Nagoya 62 mi (100 km)

To Tokyo 62 mi (100 km)

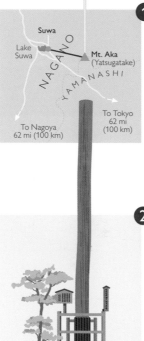

1 YAMADASHI (April)
Sixteen 200-year-old fir trees are cut down on Mt. Aka (the highest peak of the volcanic group Yatsugatake) and hauled to **Suwa** some 12.5 mi (20 km) away.

The trip takes three days. On the way, the logs have to descend a **particularly steep hill.**

With Suwa citizens aboard the logs, teams of local men drag them to the top of the hill until the logs tip over and start careening down the steep slope.

2 SATOBIKI (May)
The 16 logs are paraded through the streets of Suwa, and ceremoniously placed at each corner of the **four Shinto shrines,** replacing the logs from the previous Onbashira.

As well as riding (and falling off) the logs while they speed down the hill during Yamadashi, young men from Suwa cling to the logs while they are being raised into their final upright positions. This has caused fatal accidents during past celebrations.

In addition to log-riding and the religious aspects of the two-month long **Onbashira celebrations,** there are exhibitions of traditional drumming and dancing. Thousands of tourists come to watch.

It's difficult to stay on the logs as they descend; many riders fall off. Some of them are injured badly (some die)…

but plenty of other young men, keen to prove their bravery, try to jump onto the speeding 12 US t (10 t) monsters before they reach the bottom of the hill.

Medical help is on stand-by.

Isu-1*
Grand Prix
Office chair
racing

Japan

Kyōtanabe,
Kyoto, Japan
March

This Grand Prix was started in 2010 as a marketing stunt for a shopping arcade. Office chair racing is now popular in many parts of Japan.

Isu = chair

Elbow pads, knee pads, and **helmets** are mandatory.

Teams of three compete in the event: a two-hour **endurance race** around a course of 590 ft (180 m).

Chairs must be unmodified, off-the-shelf, standard items.

First prize is 198 lb (90 kg) of long-grain rice.

You can **face forwards** or **backwards**; or a combination of the two, swiveling as you go.

For several years, a precursor to the Japanese event has taken place in **Bad König, Germany.** In this version, two people race against each other down a 560 ft (170 m) hill with obstacles, at up to 22 mph (35 km/h).

Unlike Japan's race, **customization is allowed** (no motorized help, though). This results in barely recognizable chairs, and the fastest participants often lie face-down on their reengineered vehicles. Prizes are awarded for **best costume,** and **fastest time.**

Saidai-ji Eyo Hadaka Matsuri
Naked man festival

Saidai-ji Temple, Okayama, Japan
February

A 500-year-old festival that takes place in many locations in Japan. The most famous of these is in Okayama, and usually in cold weather, which makes it all the odder.

9,000 men, wearing nothing but traditional white loincloths, fight to catch **lucky sticks** thrown by a priest from a window high above them.

200

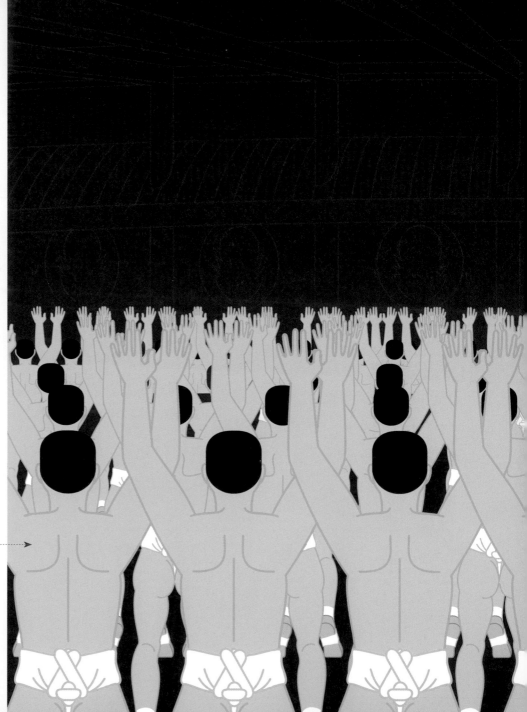

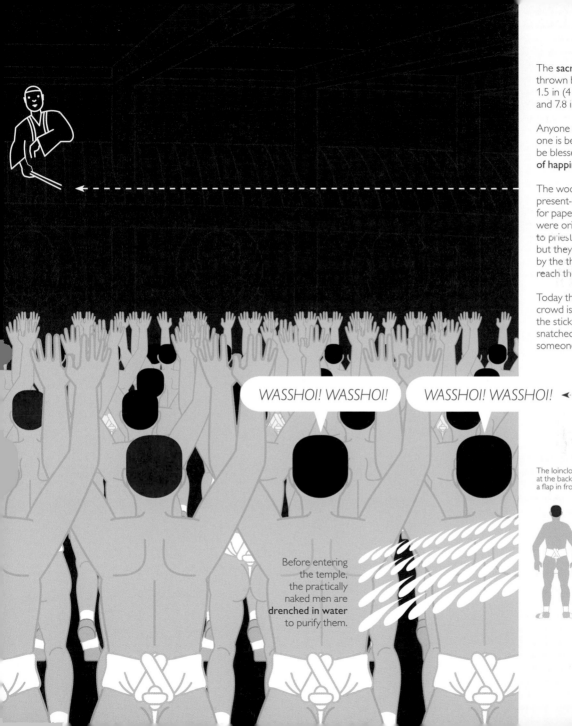

The **sacred sticks** (*shingi*) thrown by the priest are 1.5 in (4 cm) in diameter and 7.8 in (20 cm) long.

Anyone who catches one is believed to be blessed with a **year of happiness**.

The wooden sticks are present-day replacements for paper talismans that were originally distributed to priests-in-training, but they were easily torn by the throng trying to reach them.

Today the fervor of the crowd is even greater, and the sticks are liable to be snatched away as soon as someone gets hold of one.

WASSHOI! WASSHOI!

WASSHOI! WASSHOI!

Before the sticks are thrown, the men shout this popular Japanese festival chant, which expresses the desire for peacful collaboration so they can achieve goals together.

The loincloth is knotted at the back, but there's a flap in front. Thankfully.

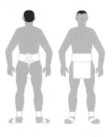

Before entering the temple, the practically naked men are **drenched in water** to purify them.

201

Kumo Gassen
Fighting spiders

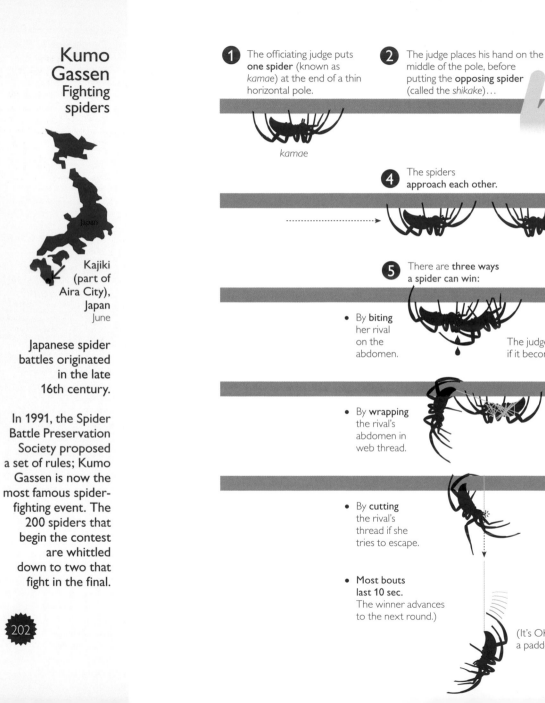

Japan

Kajiki
(part of
Aira City),
Japan
June

Japanese spider
battles originated
in the late
16th century.

In 1991, the Spider
Battle Preservation
Society proposed
a set of rules; Kumo
Gassen is now the
most famous spider-
fighting event. The
200 spiders that
begin the contest
are whittled
down to two that
fight in the final.

202

1 The officiating judge puts **one spider** (known as *kamae*) at the end of a thin horizontal pole.

kamae

2 The judge places his hand on the middle of the pole, before putting the **opposing spider** (called the *shikake*)…

4 The spiders **approach each other.**

5 There are **three ways a spider can win:**

- By **biting** her rival on the abdomen.

The judge will stop the fight if it becomes too bloody.

- By **wrapping** the rival's abdomen in web thread.

- By **cutting** the rival's thread if she tries to escape.

- Most bouts last **10 sec.** The winner advances to the next round.)

(It's OK, she lands on a padded platform.)

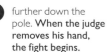

3 further down the
pole. **When the judge
removes his hand,
the fight begins.**

shikake

The bamboo fighting pole is 24 in (60 cm) long.

**There are spider
battles in many other
Asian countries,** including Korea, Malaysia,
Singapore, Thailand, and
the Philippines, where it's
been linked to gambling
addiction and to childen
getting bad grades in
school. (No gambling is
allowed at the Kajiki event.)

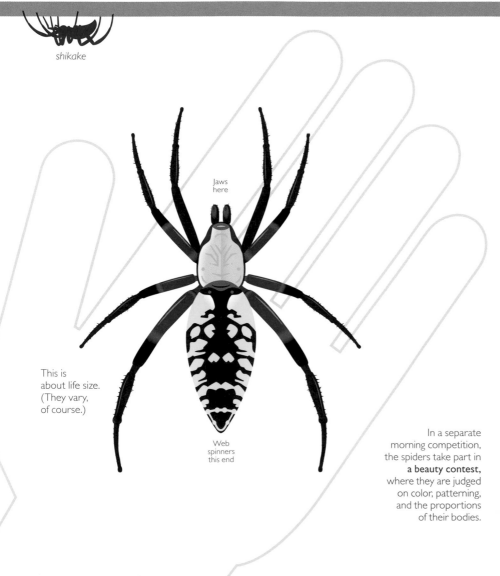

Jaws
here

This is
about life size.
(They vary,
of course.)

Web
spinners
this end

The spiders competing
in Kumo Gassen are
from the genus *Argiope*.
All have yellow markings
on their bodies, and **all
are female.** The people
of Kajiki raise the spiders
to be fighters and give
them the nickname
Samurai Spiders. Locals
allow them to make
cobwebs wherever they
like in their houses.
(Must be hard for those
who are particularly
house-proud.)

In a separate
morning competition,
the spiders take part in
a beauty contest,
where they are judged
on color, patterning,
and the proportions
of their bodies.

Beer Can Regatta

Australia

Mindil Beach,
Darwin, Australia
June

When it started
in 1974, around
60 boats competed.
At that time it
was a genuine race
with outboard
motors attached
to rafts and boats
made from cans, but
now the winner is
usually the one who
stays afloat longest.

In 1978, the
organization of the
regatta was
handed over to
the Darwin Lions
Club, and they've
run it ever since.

Part of the fun is seeing
boats come apart in the water.
One important
boat-building
tip: tape up
all open
holes!

During the 1980s,
beer companies
started making cans
out of **aluminum**
instead of steel.
Unfortunately, the
new, softer aluminum
cans could not withstand
the speeds at which
outboard motors had
driven the steel-can
boats, so now all boats
are powered by hand.

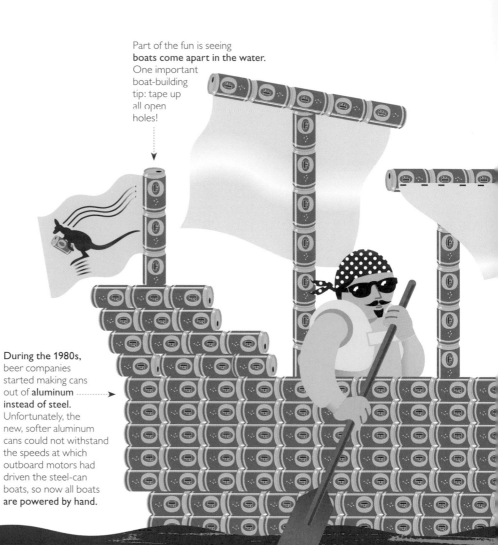

Prizes are awarded for:

 Best Soft Drink Can Boat

Best Beer Can Boat

Best Novelty Boat

(And for all races and other events)

THE RULES
The organizers issue the
10 Can-mandments. They include:

Thou shalt enter the event in the right spirit.

Thou shalt build craft from recycled cans (or milk cartons, or plastic bottles).

The craft shall float by cans alone.

Thou shalt not drown.

Other competitions during the regatta:

- Men's and women's **Thong Throwing** (Note: these are thongs worn on the feet, not the other kind.)

- Men's and women's **Tug of War**

- Children's **Sandcastle Building**

- Children's **Kayak Racing**

- Iron Man and **Iron Women**

- **The Battle of Mindil** a sort of underwater treasure hunt

- **Henley on Mindil** a race for non-seaworthy craft (You carry the "boat" and run like mad along the beach.)

Australia Day Cockroach Races

Australia

Brisbane, Australia
January 26

This event started in **1982** in the parking lot of the Story Bridge Hotel in Brisbane, following a beer-fueled discussion about who had the fastest cockroaches.

Actual average size of an adult cockroach.
Lifespan: up to two years.

Competing cockroaches—usually referred to as "cockies"—are numbered on the back before each race (not easy). You can bring your own, or buy them for AUD 5 on race day. There's an entry fee of the same price for each cocky and there are 13 races. All proceeds go to charity.

The races are over in seconds. This is because cockroaches move at 50 body lengths per second, equivalent to a sprinter running at 200 mph (322 km/h) and covering 328 ft (100 m) in 1 sec.

So, **if a world-class sprinter and a cockroach** of the same length ran a 328 ft (100 m) race, the roach would cross the finish line in 1 sec, while the sprinter would only have covered 34.4 ft (10.5 m).

0 ft (0 m)	34.4 ft (10.5 m) Sprinter running for 1 sec	164 ft (50 m)

The MC announces the name and number of each cocky before every race.

A few names from the Cocky Hall of Fame:

Alfred Hitchcocky
Irish Cock
Osama Bin Liner
Priscilla Queen of the Dr
Cocky Dundee
Soft Cocky

3 m (10 ft)

Roaches not drawn to scale.

In some races a garden hose is used as an obstacle.

Official rules say that if spectators step inside the yellow Olde Canvasse, they'll be fined AUD 100,000,000.

Although Brisbane's Australia Day races are considered **the gold standard of the cockroach calendar,** other races are held in different parts of the country, as well as in the US.

Races start when the roaches (up to 40) are released from the center of the arena. The first to reach the perimeter is the winner.

Four stewards determine the winner as well as the ones in second and third place. The judgment cannot be challenged.

Pipers and drummers circle the arena before each race (often playing "Waltzing Matilda").

Following the band there's a steward with **competitors** in a glass jar.

328 ft (100 m)
Cockroach running
for 1 sec

Tuna Toss
World
Championships

Australia

**Port Lincoln,
Australia**
January 26
(Australia Day)

In **1979**, the
organizers of
Tunarama, an
annual festival
celebrating the
Australian
fishing industry,
were looking
for a unique
way to spice up
their festivities.

Tuna fishermen had always unloaded their
catch by throwing fish from the boats
onto waiting trucks. It seemed like this
was the obvious choice for a
competitive and fun event.

Competitors
realized pretty quickly that
they could toss the tuna
farther if they used a **classic
hammer-throwing
technique.**

In 1998, Australian hammer thrower Sean Carlin threw a tuna **122 ft (37.2 m),** and this still stands as the world record. The women's record is held by Brooke Krueger (also a hammer thrower). In 2002 she tossed a tuna 69.9 ft (21.3 m).

Weight equality
In order to make sure that everyone is throwing the same weight, 20 lb (9 kg) **rubberized models** of the fish were eventually substituted for the real thing in the competition's first rounds. However, **in the final rounds, real (but dead*) tuna are still tossed.**

* See **La Batalla de Ratas** (p. 114) in which dead rats are thrown in Spain. It seems that throwing all sorts of stuff is popular worldwide; for instance, **La Tomatina** (p. 112), also in Spain, and **Mobile Phones** (p. 140) in Finland.

Golden Shears
World Shearing and Woolhandling Championship

New Zealand

**Masterton,
New Zealand**
March

The first Golden Shears competition was held in 1961. At that time it was just a New Zealand thing; it became the World Shearing Championship in 1980. Woolhandling and woolpressing were added in 1996.

There are **three competitions** in the Golden Shears event. Most are divided into four or five **different proficiency categories,** allowing anyone from novice to full-time worker to compete at the appropriate level.

1 SHEARING
A shearer who can fleece more than 200 sheep a day is called a **gun shearer.** (Really good ones can shear 400-plus sheep a day.) These experts take part in the **Open Final,** which draws the championship's largest crowd of spectators.

Most shearers use the **Bowen technique,** developed in New Zealand. It details a preferred order of cuts, and a way of handling the animal so that it is as relaxed as possible. Fleeces are shorn in about 50 sec.

The points system: during the shearing, one point is counted for every 20 sec taken, while judges allot performance penalty points. When the shorn sheep are returned to their pens, judges add further penalty points for cuts, damaged fleece, and any wool left on the animal. **The lowest score wins.**

First the belly hair is cut off, then the whole of one side, in a series of long, smooth cuts (called blows). The sheep is turned over and the other side is shorn, **leaving a large part of the fleece in one piece.**

Halfway through, the animal would look like this, if it was standing up. (All the cutting is actually done with the sheep on its back or side.)

In general, a sheep is shorn once a year.

② WOOL HANDLING

Two sheep are shorn (not competitively in this event) for each wool handler, whose job is to **sort the wool into various grades.** This is often, but not always, performed by women. They throw the fleece onto a slatted wool table and pick off inferior pieces. (Small bits that fall through the slats onto the floor are used for the outside of tennis balls.) **The fleeces are folded** up and put into bags for pressing.

One point is counted for every 5 sec taken, and penalty points are added for any remaining inferior wool that might detract from the fleece's value at sale.

③ WOOL PRESSING

This is the process of making the wool into **bales** for transport.

First, wool is packed into two containers—one called the top box and the other the bottom box, with the latter having a canvas liner in it. The top box is cranked up so it sits on top of the bottom box and the presser operates a winch to compress the wool from the top box into the bottom one.

Finally, the presser folds and secures the liner and releases the bale.

The competition is largely about **speed.** It takes an experienced presser about 9 min to make a 243 lb (110 kg) tightly packed and bound bale.

Sheep shearing used to be done with **clippers** like these.

They are still used in places where slow, traditional methods are valued (or where there's no electricity).

The **cutting device used at Golden Shears** is an amped-up version of the electrical shaver you use on your face, or legs.

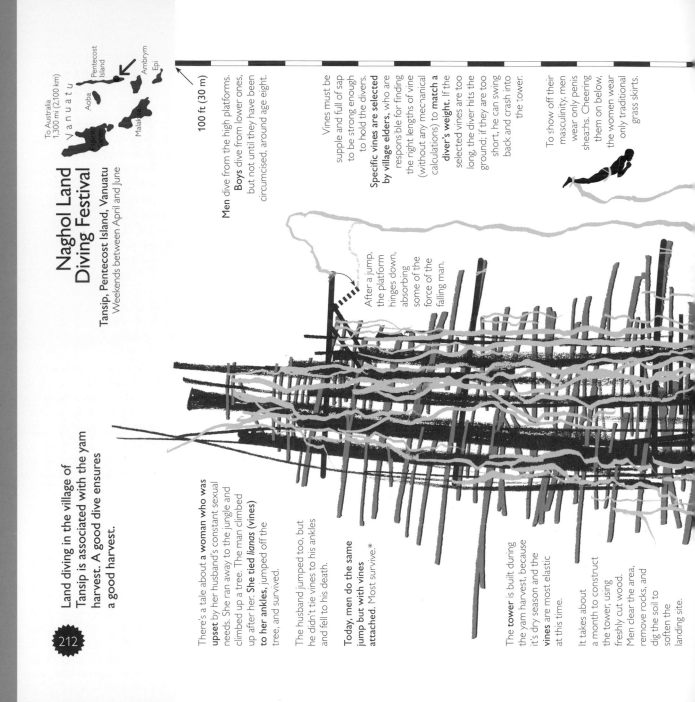

Naghol Land Diving Festival

Tansip, Pentecost Island, Vanuatu
Weekends between April and June

Land diving in the village of Tansip is associated with the yam harvest. A good dive ensures a good harvest.

To Australia
1,300 mi (2,100 km)

V a n u a t u
Aoba   Pentecost Island
Espiritu Santo
Malakula   Ambrym
Epi

100 ft (30 m)

Men dive from the high platforms. **Boys** dive from lower ones, but not until they have been circumcised, around age eight.

Vines must be supple and full of sap to be strong enough to hold the divers. **Specific vines are selected by village elders,** who are responsible for finding the right lengths of vine (without any mechanical calculations) to **match a diver's weight.** If the selected vines are too long, the diver hits the ground; if they are too short, he can swing back and crash into the tower.

To show off their masculinity, men wear only penis sheaths. Cheering them on below, the women wear only traditional grass skirts.

After a jump, the platform hinges down, absorbing some of the force of the falling man.

There's a tale about **a woman who was upset** by her husband's constant sexual needs. She ran away to the jungle and climbed up a tree. The man climbed up after her. **She tied** *lianas* **(vines) to her ankles,** jumped off the tree, and survived.

The husband jumped too, but he didn't tie the vines to his ankles and fell to his death.

Today, men do the same jump but with vines attached. Most survive.*

The **tower** is built during the yam harvest, because it's dry season and the **vines** are most elastic at this time.

It takes about a month to construct the tower, using freshly cut wood. Men clear the area, remove rocks, and dig the soil to soften the landing site.

During the dive, men plummet to the ground at speeds of up to 45 mph (72 km/h).

In the best jumps, the diver tucks his chin to his chest and lands close to the ground, just brushing his shoulders on the soil. The higher the platform he jumps from, the better the yam harvest will be.

In 1995, Pentecost islanders started to press for royalties from bungee-jumping companies.

*Only one death has been recorded since 1974. It was during a visit to Pentecost Island by **Queen Elizabeth II**, who wanted to see a dive. The man had a good luck charm with him when he jumped. Since then jumpers have not carried good luck charms.

Thank you

My friend **Julius Wiedemann** took the idea for this book to his boss **Benedikt Taschen,** who to my surprise said yes. Thank you, *obrigado, danke sehr,* Julius, for all your encouragement, and your patience with my impatience about all sorts of things as the book progressed.

Julius was the book's editor, but **Erin,** my long-suffering wife, was my editor. You were always there to make constructive comments on the pages, to correct ideas that were clearly misguided, and at the end of the day to make the best martinis known to gin drinkers. (Thank you to Hendricks, Uncle Val's, and Bombay Sapphire. If you see this advertisement, you might restock my gin supply. Or just send money.)

A heartfelt thank you to **Nora Dohrmann** and **Stefan Klatte** at TASCHEN, who were terrific, calm collators of my files. While Nora coordinated the many different tasks, Stefan—the unsung hero of the project—converted everything from Freehand MX to Adobe Illustrator. It's a long story, but perhaps one day Freehand will be recognized as the most intuitive vector-based illustration tool ever made, and will be restored to full and proper support.

Chris Mizsak and **Gill Paul** gathered information and links and painstakingly checked everything, including spelling, grammar, and website updatedness

(including words like updatedness.) **Jürgen Dubau, Anja Lenze** and **Maike Specht** then took care that everything made sense in German. The team at **Delivering iBooks & Design** did the same for French. *Danke sehr* and *merci beaucoup!*

Thank you **Rowland** for invaluable and always available technical advice. You taught me that my computer is not actually my enemy, and that sudden problems can be sorted out by calmly following along as you, in far-off Italy, walk me through the steps to restore the maddening but wonderful machine to working order again. (Of course I thank you for a whole lot more!) A big loving hug for my son.

Lots of friends told me about their favourite odd events. **Frank Halloran** was particularly insistent that I consider a number of Spanish ones, and his general enthusiasm from the start of the project buoyed me. *Muchas gracias,* Frank.

To everyone who invited me to dine, or go somewhere, or party with them during the past year—invitations that I turned down (I hope politely)—please forgive me. Here's the reason.

214

Biography

Last but not least, a few words about me, I am a **British-American graphic designer** who spent **16 years at _Time_ magazine,** eventually becoming its graphics director. Always at the sharp end of information graphics, my clients have included **Apple, Sony,** _National Geographic,_ and _The New York Times._ I have also authored and contributed to **several books** on the subject, and **taught at Stanford** and presented at **TED Conferences.** I believe in the **power of humor** to help people understand stuff, and I always wear blue.

Imprint

EACH AND EVERY TASCHEN BOOK PLANTS A SEED!
TASCHEN is a carbon neutral publisher. Each year, we offset our annual carbon emissions with carbon credits at the Instituto Terra, a reforestation program in Minas Gerais, Brazil, founded by Lélia and Sebastião Salgado. To find out more about this ecological partnership, please check: www.taschen.com/zerocarbon.
Inspiration: unlimited.
Carbon footprint: zero.

To stay informed about TASCHEN and our upcoming titles, please subscribe to our free magazine at www.taschen.com/magazine, follow us on Twitter, Instagram, and Facebook, or e-mail your questions to contact@taschen.com.

p. 34: special thanks to todayifoundout.com and talklikeapirate.com
p. 57: portrait of Anne Woods drawn from a photo by John Angerson/Rex
p. 156: silhouette based on a photograph by Eric Lafforgue

Editor in charge
Julius Wiedemann

Editorial coordination
Nora Dorhmann

Collaboration
Daniel Siciliano Brêtas

Research and fact-checking
Chris Mizsak

Editing
Gill Paul

Proofreading
Delivering iBooks & Design, Barcelona

Production
Stefan Klatte

Printed in Italy
ISBN 978-3-8365-3908-1